Country Fried Soul

ADVENTURES IN DIRTY SOUTH HIP★HOP

TAMARA PALMER

Country Fried Soul

ADVENTURES IN DIRTY SOUTH HIP★HOP

Tamara Palmer

A BACKBEAT BOOK

First edition 2005

Published by Backbeat Books

600 Harrison Street

San Francisco, CA 94107, USA

www.backbeatbooks.com

An imprint of The Music Player Network, United Entertainment Media Inc.

Published for Backbeat Books by Outline Press Ltd,

2A Union Court, 20-22 Union Road, London SW4 6JP, England

www.backbeatuk.com

ISBN 0-87930-857-5

EDITOR John Morrish

DESIGN Paul Cooper Design

Origination by Solidity Graphics and Print by Colorprint Offset (Hong Kong)

05 06 07 08 09 5 4 3 2 1

Country Fried Soul

ADVENTURES IN DIRTY SOUTH HIP*HOP

Goodie Mob: pioneers of Southern rap – and still in business after more than a decade.

CONTENTS
★ FOREWORD BY DAVID BANNER

a-side

b-side

David Banner: "If you listen to Southern music, it's the most honest music in the world."

FOREWORD

By David Banner

I always connect the South with a diamond. Do you know what a diamond is derived from? It's derived from a piece of coal. A piece of coal that out of a million pieces of coal, when it went through the fire, right before incineration, it tucked its nuts and stayed strong and held fast. When it healed it became the most priceless element on Earth, which is a diamond. And that's how I look at the South.

People always use the term "keep it real" and I would always say as far as the South is concerned that I never want to keep it real. Because what's real is my people are hurting and when I think of the South I think of pain and struggle. But through pain and struggle is how you grow.

If you listen to Southern music, it's the most honest music in the world. Because Southern rappers are the only people that can tell you that they're weak and still be the hardest rapper in the world. It's the same person who in one song can talk about God and talk about the club in the same sentence. And when people look at it they say that it's a contradiction, but it's actually not. It's true life. It's honest life, because half of the people who are in church on Sunday still smell like Hennessy from the night before. But we mean it and it's not a joke; it's just how we live.

Lil Jon screaming on a hook ain't about rapping, it's a feeling. It's like going to church. It's a spirit. That's why they can't understand why Lil Jon is selling how he's selling. Lil Jon's music is the grunge music for black kids. The way that Kurt Cobain made kids feel when he came out yelling, 'Teen Spirit.' The same way when Pastor Troy tells them that 'We Ready,' or T.I. talking about 'Trap Muzik,' or when 8Ball and MJG talk about 'Memphis City Blues,' or when David Banner's talking about Mississippi. That's something that a person would never be able to understand. It's a feeling. There's nothing that can be explained in words. If it could be explained in words, corporate America would take it and put it in Vanilla Ice and put him back out.

I look at the South as being a summation of all music. If you look at it, the foundation of all or most contemporary music in America is the blues. And then after that it would be jazz, and that derived from Mississippi and Alabama. James Brown from Georgia was rapping before rap was rap.

What existed before hip-hop was blues music, and it came from my people. So when you look at hip-hop as a whole it has finally made its full turn and is full circle.

If you even go back to your samples in New York rap, one of the most sampled sounds in hip-hop breaks comes from a group called Freedom and they're from Jackson, Mississippi. James Brown is straight from the South. There are all these groups that people sampled and made millions of records off, these are all Southern records. But we never get credit for it.

I just thank God that I have an opportunity to make kids where I'm from feel like they're somebody. Because every time they see David Banner on TV, every time they see that Mississippi tattooed across my back, they feel like they can make it too. And now kids from Mississippi will hold their chests up when they try to make it in the rap world.

What I want people to know is, you only have a minute and you will be judged by the things you do in that minute. The thing that I hope that I can do is put the slaves to rest. All the souls and all the old blues singers and all the people that didn't get that opportunity and for all those people that have voices.

I think Southern hip-hop, in everything we do and everything we say, it comes back to love. And I think love's twin brother or love within itself is pain. Because the only reason why you love something is because it has an ability to hurt us.

All the stuff we talk about in our music is pain, whether we want to admit it or not, from the hoes in the club to the shooting and the busting to diamonds on our hands. We shine because we felt so bad for so long. Our self-esteem was beaten into the ground from slavery up until now. So we shine to make ourselves feel better. We put the gold in our mouth to shield us from that pain. And I think that's why people feel Southern music so much.

Born Lavell Crump in Mississippi, the artist known as David Banner is an insightful rapper, in-demand producer, record label owner, and selfless activist. First making a splash nationally as part of the duo Crooked Lettaz in the late 1990s, he released the solo album Them Firewater Boyz Vol. 1 *independently in 2000. In early 2003, Banner and his b.i.G.f.a.c.e Entertainment signed a deal valued at $10m with Universal Records.*

Banner's most recent albums, Mississippi: The Album *and* MTA2: Baptized in Dirty Water, *have thrown light on his state, home to the nation's lowest per capita income and highest struggle. His songs, which depict the range of emotion of true life in the South, have put him and Mississippi forever on the hip-hop map and garnered both critical and popular praise.*

A graduate of Southern University, David Banner is presently working on music and plans for building a community center in Jackson, Mississippi.

INTRODUCTION

Pause Button Dynamics

FEATURING **Teemoney**

"Let this be an example … Originality works for those who have the patience to wait."
– *FROM LINER NOTES OF BIG GIPP'S MUTANT MINDFRAME ALBUM*

[Record]

Should have known that my bright idea to make a mixtape in book form was also kind of doomed.

[Stop], [Rewind], [Play]

It made good sense at first. As a matter of fact, it seemed like the perfect approach for a book that aimed to open a window onto the world of the Dirty South by sampling of different voices and topics related to the music and culture. As both a DJ (recently as Teemoney) and writer for the past 12 years, I almost always apply the same cut-and-paste technique to creating feature stories as I do to mixing records.

So what could be a better way of creating my first book, especially one as music and DJ-centric as this? The simple answer is *anything else*. Why? Well, I forgot one really vital thing about making mixtapes: It's fucking difficult.

If you take pride in displaying your DJ skills to their full potential, making mixtapes is insanely tedious. The quest for perfection is ripe. There are millions of potential mistakes, both big and small, and all of them will instantly stop the show.

Little vinyl pop right when you lay the needle down? Start over.
Tiny skip in the track, 45 minutes into the mix? Start over.
Start a tune at the wrong time? Start over.
Two songs with wildly clashing keys? Start over.
Breathe wrong on the record or look at it funny? Sorry. Over.
Throw the crossfader onto the wrong channel? *Aaand* take it from the top.
Mismatch the beats, producing an Amtrak-sized trainwreck? Pack it up!

Of course, today they have these devices called computers, which run software that can neatly and conveniently make digital recordings in which all mistakes can be edited out later with a couple of mouse clicks. And CD players instead of turntables eliminate the pesky snaps and crackles that come with records. Thus, there's a legion of DJ-mixed CDs on the market remarkably free of technical errors. What talented DJs! (Yeah, right.)

Take it back to the essence and keep it gutter, fingers in the trenches of the vinyl grooves with the tape winding around, and making a mixtape is not going to be such an effortless process. If any single generalisation can be made about the pioneers and torch carriers of Southern hip-hop, it's that they haven't traveled the easy road to the heights and successes they currently enjoy, with gold, platinum and multi-platinum honors. So why should I take the expressway in attempting to write about it? It's best to take the slow, scenic route instead.

Imagine being a DJ charged with the task of making a mix that educates and entertains people while giving them a snapshot of a scene. You might get started easily enough, but it's not long before amazing records keep dropping in your lap, one after the other. There are so many that you can barely concentrate, let alone breathe, as black wax piles up over you. All the records may have some small thread running through them, but the sounds are as varied as can be, from a mellow cosmic alien love song like 'Prototype' from Andre 3000 of multi-platinum superstars OutKast to the paranoid schizophrenic hallucinations of rough ghetto life portrayed in Geto Boys' 'Mind Playin Tricks On Me.'

Put that in the context of writing a book and it all goes haywire. For if the Dirty South (which, by the way, grabs its name from a song by the influential group Goodie Mob) ever had a time in the sun, that time is now, and it is burning hot and bright. There's an avalanche of soul-stirring, body-bumping music infiltrating the mainstream airwaves that tried to deny it for so long, taking charge after years of struggling to be heard.

Legendary Southern artist MJG (Marlon Jermaine Goodwin), best known for his long-time partnership with Premro Smith as 8Ball & MJG, has an easy explanation for the well-earned success the South now enjoys. "Sometimes you work harder or run harder when you've been held back," he offers.

[Stop], [Rewind], [Play]

In my soul I've been a DJ for much longer than the 12 years I officially claim. It dates back close to a blasted quarter century.

Back then I'd make tapes with my late great uncle, a songwriter by hobby who penned the first jingle for the refreshing beverage we call 7Up. His name was Roy B. Black, which was kinda funny because in actuality, we be Jewish (thank you, I'll be here all week). We had a fictional radio station called KTAM and we would record commentary in between songs, mainly by The Beatles, which we had a lot of around the house. Later it was the synth pop I was taping off the local Bay Area radio: Human League, Eurythmics, Thompson Twins.

Around age 12, I would sit on the floor in my parents' kitchen and make tapes with the record player and the tape recorder. Using the pause button on the tape recorder, I'd grab snatches of sounds, words and phrases from different records, pinning them down together on the cassette in a giant sound collage.

I saw Grandmaster Flash on television, standing behind his incredible wheels of steel and scratching records, but didn't dare try it at home. It seemed much too dangerous, especially since only some of the records were mine.

It might take hours to get even a minute of good tape using these pause button dynamics, but the reward was always in the results. Because really, how else would Frankie Goes To Hollywood and The Cure get in the same space to jam and get funky with Prince and Michael Jackson?

At the time, I was into the tedium of making tapes. Frankly, that was a big part of the thrill. Nowadays, when I have to rewind and re-record so much it brews frustration and insecurity.

Chalk it up to too much good material, but the Dirty South sure is running things right now when it comes to innovative music and human interest stories behind the beats. Try cramming all that into a mixtape, even one with a little space to stretch out and breathe.

The other big problem with using a mixtape approach to writing a book is that it brings the importance of the audience even more into the forefront. After all, astute listeners, as well as readers, can pick out mistakes on instinct. I'm speaking from experience, as someone whose body will stop cold on a dancefloor when the DJ starts trainwrecking beats. Can't help it – it's a physiological response.

But, challenge is good. So long as everyone understands that what you hold in your hands is more a lovingly sampladelic oral history than a linear academic textbook about the Dirty South, no feelings should be hurt. When those books eventually do come out, they should – and hopefully will – be written by authors who have been in the trenches for years, grinding right alongside the artists and labels for all of America to notice what's going on down South.

As a fan of Southern hip-hop, my goal here is to help share some of its flavor and an insight into the people who make it tick, sparking either a new or deeper interest in this music for those who have read about it.

If an artist or label is not mentioned here, it's not necessarily because they didn't have something to contribute. I'm just a fan making a tape of music that I love, and there's enough inspiration and quality material for several tapes. Since this is a mix, the reader should feel free to remix it: Rewind and fast forward as desired, reading chapters in any order that appeals.

Someone – many credit Frank Zappa, others Elvis Costello – once said, "Writing about music is like dancing about architecture." And it has a grain of truth – I say only a grain, or else I'd be out of a job. There is no real substitute for taking in the music itself. People who already know and love these sounds will easily be able to conjure up a soundtrack to these chapters, whether in their mind or through their own music collection. And those who might be looking for some specific musical recommendations will find plenty of suggestions in the book's B-Side.

[Stop], [Rewind], [Record]

Welcome to the *Adventures*. This mixtape is for us.

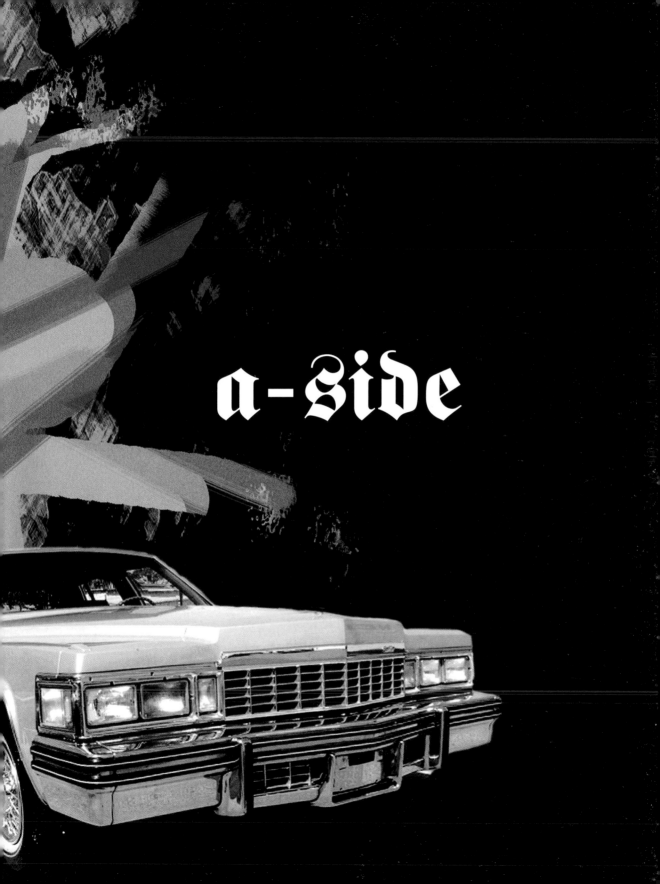

FOUNDATIONS

FEATURING **Luther Campbell, 8Ball & MJG and Too $hort**

"The South got something to say. That's all I got to say."
– ANDRE 3000 OF OUTKAST, RESPONDING TO A CHORUS OF BOOS WHILE ACCEPTING THE AWARD FOR BEST NEW ARTIST AT THE SOURCE AWARDS, 1995

That night in New York, OutKast felt low on support as discontent rang out all around them. 10 years later, OutKast have an international audience at rapt attention, as do a growing number of artists from the South.

Atlanta's dynamic duo (Andre 'Andre 3000' Benjamin and Antwan 'Big Boi' Patton) have spent the last few years racking up awards. Not just in music, by the way. They've gotten the traditional Grammys and American Music Awards (and pretty much every other type of music award), but there have also been awards such as the "Sexiest Vegetarian" and "Best Dressed" honors, given to Andre 3000 in 2004 by activist group People for the Ethical Treatment of Animals and men's magazine *GQ*, respectively. The most recent OutKast release *Speakerboxx/The Love Below* sold more than nine million copies in a year.

In a way, OutKast's music eloquently describes the range of possibility in Southern hip-hop – almost as if Big Boi and Andre 3000 were giant quotation marks bookending a richly diverse poem. Big Boi has honed his style to speak directly to the streets with car trunk funk and razor-sharp lyrical prowess. Meanwhile, Andre 3000 is more of a musical free spirit, wandering from cloud to cloud, picking up different instruments and sounds along the way, from techno and rock to love songs and hymns.

OutKast are at the forefront of what is now recognized as a genuine musical movement. Looking in from the outside, life seems pretty good for hip-hop from the South these days. The last decade has seen artists and labels from the region break records and set new standards for record contract negotiation.

Master P (Percy Miller), a rapper/hip-hop entrepreneur from New Orleans, was influenced by West Coast gangsta rap from people like Oakland's Too $hort and LA's Ice T and N.W.A. (Niggaz With Attitudes), the group that featured the now well known rapper/actor Ice Cube and rapper/producer Dr. Dre. For a few years P even operated his own independent store, No Limit Records, in Richmond, a rough town in the San Francisco Bay Area.

Just three years after Master P impressed industry pundits by signing a valuable distribution deal with heavyweight Priority Records for his No Limit label in 1995, another New Orleans label, Cash Money Records, secured a sweeter deal with a larger company. Cash Money would be distributed by Universal and receive an even bigger paycheck: $30m, the largest deal of its kind at the time.

While this sort of business success was hard to disrespect, there were still vocal critics of the street sounds coming from the No Limit and Cash Money camps (particularly the former), which were deemed unsophisticated and uninspiring by some. Whatever one's opinion, they were far enough removed from the musical adventures of OutKast that rarely were they all lumped together as the giant, varied Southern scene that was actually happening from Texas to Florida and everywhere in between.

And then came a DJ/producer named Lil Jon, ambassador for a movement called crunk, both an intense club sound and a supercharged way of life that had been bubbling over among young people in Atlanta. Channeling this energy, Lil Jon was giving people something they could *feel*.

> **and then came a dj/producer named lil jon, ambassador for a movement called crunk**

On *Slanguistics*, a special on the MTV2 cable network, Andre 3000 offered a succinct analogy for crunk. "What punk was to rock," he explains, "crunk is to rap."

With bass-heavy tones and 808 drum machine rhythms influenced by the electro-funk of New Yorker Afrika Bambaataa's 'Planet Rock' as well as the most hot-stepping riddims firing out of Jamaican dancehalls and the call and response chants popularized in the Atlanta and Miami bass scenes, Lil Jon's records struck a chord that resonated in party people from the underground to the mainstream.

Following his lead were a host of artists – a great many produced by Lil Jon himself – helping to certify the movement and prove their worth as entertainers and business people in the international arena. As the Lil Jon hits stacked up, so did confidence that the South had truly arrived. *Vibe*, a national magazine traditionally known for focusing on its East Coast roots, estimated that songs from Southern artists garnered more exposure than any other region on urban radio in 2004, with nearly 44 per cent of the year's top airplay. And a quick peek at the gold and platinum sales certificates from the Recording Industry Association of America (RIAA) shows that the South has also claimed a large share of hip-hop's plaques in recent years.

It's clearly a good time for the Dirty South. So why do the artists and labels that make it tick sometimes still feel like hip-hop's version of Rodney Dangerfield, whose famous catchphrase was 'I don't get no respect.'?

I'm sweating in the afternoon sun in front of Gloria Estefan's Cuban restaurant on

17

the world-famous Ocean Drive in South Beach, Miami. Just across the street are the healthy green palm trees, intense blue water and white sand beach made internationally famous by numerous hip-hop videos. Shortly after arriving, I'm joined by Luther Campbell, also known as Uncle Luke and, until George Lucas got mad in the early 1990s and slapped him with a cease-and-desist order, Luke Skyywalker of 2 Live Crew fame.

He doesn't always get credit for it because of his hedonistic sexual content, but Luke remains one of hip-hop's pre-eminent freedom fighters. He famously defended his right to free speech when 2 Live Crew's album *As Nasty As They Wanna Be* (1989) was declared legally obscene. He fought a Florida court ruling all the way up to the Supreme Court – and won the right to carry on with his music, a bone-rattling, lascivious club sound known as 'bass,' which was also taking hold in Atlanta, thanks to people like MC Shy D and DJ Smurf. Luke also battled long and hard

> it would be the better part of a decade before southern hip-hop was recognized as a movement

for the South to be respected on a national level, shouting and yelling and sometimes even busting ass to make sure he was getting the point across.

Luke and I start by talking about how the South is so successful right now in music and entertainment. Artists are getting considered for Hollywood roles, enjoying a fair share of attention in hip-hop magazines, garnering endorsements, creating their own products and setting business precedents.

He's not that impressed, though, and utters one word: "Default." There's no smile on his face. A few minutes later, he clarifies.

"The South – remember when I said by default? I always predicted this, but nobody really wanted this to become a reality. It gets real deep. Even to this day right now, the South is really not respected."

Hard to imagine now that OutKast have been anything but loved by everyone. The jeers at The Source Awards in 1995 weren't directed entirely towards the group. It was also symbolic of how a vocal part of the music industry in New York, the city that claims to be Ground Zero for hip-hop, felt about what they saw as the South's attempts to steal the spotlight.

Andre 3000, Big Boi and dozens of other artists across the Southern states have fought exhaustively for the recognition and respect that's only begun to come their way. Their response to the negative pressure was to work hard – so hard that one day no one would be able to deny them that respect.

2 Live Crew and the Geto Boys (Houston's ghetto reality rappers Scarface, Willie D and Bushwick Bill) were among the first to lead the South into the national arena in the

late 1980s and early 1990s. It would be the better part of a decade before the regional force of Southern hip-hop was really recognized as a movement.

With national attention elsewhere and disrespect hanging thick in the air for so many years, the South had to focus inward to find success. Without the guidance and infrastructure provided by the conventional record companies in New York and Los Angeles, Southerners instead took a cue from West Coast pioneers like Too $hort and E-40 and formed their own independent record labels.

They also developed alternative methods of distributing their music, through small local record shops commonly known as 'Mom and Pop' stores and, in many cases, right out of the trunk of the car or on the street. They cut out the large-scale middle-man (ie, the established record label) to such an extent that they made more on the sale of each recording than anyone with a big contract could ever hope to see. To this day, the fundamental question posed to a successfully independent Southern rapper contemplating a major label deal is whether they want to be rich (by staying independent) or famous (by going with a major).

Most of the new generation saw how hard it was for groups like 2 Live Crew to be accepted nationally; the tales of fighting are legendary and make tackling the country sound a bit less appealing.

"I remember one time we was in St. Louis on a big New York tour, because we were probably one of the first ones to go on tour with New York artists," says Luke. "They'd make us go on last, even though we wasn't the headliners. We'd go on last and all the New York artists would leave. Normally at a hip-hop concert, everybody's on the side of the stage seeing who rocked. On the side of our stage, because they fought the promoter so hard, everybody would leave. All of 'em: Fat Boys, Salt 'N Pepa, Kid 'N Play. They'd get in their cars and leave. Go to the next city, without even looking at us. I mean, it was bananas."

Unfortunately, Luke's stories about disrespect from the East Coast-based hip-hop industry are numerous.

"I remember there was a time in Mississippi where they said, 'You all only got three minutes on stage.' Three minutes? You know what I'm saying? You don't want us on this? All New York groups, Eric B and Rakim, Run-DMC, yada yada yada – all of 'em. 'You've got three minutes on stage to open up.' We were like, three minutes on stage? Okay, this is what we're gonna do. We'll cut a Jam Master Jay record for three minutes. Fuck y'all. So we did stuff like that and then had to fight, literally had to fight. I remember beating up Public Enemy's road manager, beating the shit out of him in Savannah, Georgia, because of the same shit.

"Walking out of a concert in Missouri, going to the New Music Seminar [in New York] and they're, 'Oh that South music, it's just regional. They only sell in Miami.' Get up in front of the whole thing and say 'Fuck you.' You know, I'm talking about executives in the room. So it cuts a lot deeper with me than with a lot of other people because I lived it, I had to take the flag and I had to defend it for it to get to where it's at right now. I could sit here and tell you a million stories, you know, and then it would just be a Luke book. The situation is really deep. It's like we came through slavery days all over again. And to get it to where we're at right now, I still feel a little angry about the industry because the industry hasn't really accepted it."

Some things rarely change, it seems. The South has never been properly celebrated for its musical innovations, including its contributions to hip-hop.

Up until this point, the tale of hip-hop has been written and rewritten to mythological proportions, always with New York at the forefront of the story. And while there's no dispute as to the Big Apple's crucial role in the development of what is now the dominant youth culture of the world, there's been comparatively less discussion about the origins of the music styles that laid the groundwork for hip-hop. Maybe some people think it's easier or more accurate to slap a 'Made in New York' tag on it, but that would be a tragic miscarriage of justice.

We *could* take it all the way back to Africa, to the tribal collective spirit and the hypnotic power of the drum beat. Or we could fast forward a bit and shoot over to the shores of Jamaica, where selectors (what we now think of as DJs) outdid each other with the size and bass-rattling power of their sound systems.

But *our* story is about the South, a vital part of hip-hop's foundations, with its incredible musical inventions, from blues and jazz to soul and rock and roll. With that in mind, it shouldn't be a surprise that some of the areas that have made the most noise in Southern hip-hop –Memphis, New Orleans, Atlanta, Miami – have consistently been creative hotbeds of musical innovation dating back to the first half of the 20th century.

Once the South applied all of its musical knowledge and innovation to creating hip-hop, the results were audibly different. And it wasn't just blues or rock; with Southern hip-hop you could hear threads of gospel or even the glorious horns and rhythms of marching bands (and, specifically, the drumlines) of high schools and universities.

"For a long time hip-hop was just snippets and elements of other stuff," Mannie Fresh, producer of platinum hits for Cash Money, told *Scratch Magazine*. "But when you get to the South it actually becomes music. You have more people playing it. You got structure, you got chords, you got strings, as opposed to just taking a little snippet and doing something crazy with it. You actually got musicianship in Southern music."

In that sense, there's a larger continuity. Music is in the very air Southerners breathe from birth, as much an element of life in the South as family or faith. Today's Southern artists are just furthering their bloodlines.

"Memphis, Tennessee is a music city," explains MJG of the area he and 8Ball represent, alongside such luminaries as Al Green, Otis Redding, Booker T & the MGs, Isaac Hayes and the Bar-Kays (house musicians for the legendary Stax label). "This is the

8Ball (right) and MJG: Steeped in the music of Memphis, Tennessee.

home of the blues, birthplace of rock and roll. Here, you either know somebody or somebody's uncle, brother, daddy or somebody is a musician.

"If you truly understand and listen [to classic records], they're saying the same things – just in their time, in their way, in their day," he says. "I like listening to it too 'cos I'm trying to carry the vibe on. I want somebody somewhere listening to my CD 20 years from now and so if I give it that way, maybe I'll get it back.

"If you talk to a blues artist or R&B artist about studio time that they used to do in the '70s or '80s or whatever, it's all pretty much the same. There are a lot of studios that have been here in Memphis for a long time, 20, 30, 40 years. In fact, *we'll* be here for 20, 30 or 40 years."

People in the South were steeped in traditional music, but the radio also brought them the current hip-hop flavor from New York in the 1980s and 1990s. Though they were thousands of miles away, a generation was being raised on East Coast hip-hop just the same.

"I actually grew up on New York rappers, you know," 8Ball reveals. "Steady B and Just Ice and BDP [Boogie Down Productions] and LL Cool J and Run-DMC, stuff like that. Cats like that always preached individuality. I grew up on that type of stuff and then I started hearing stuff like [the West Coast's] Too $hort and Geto Boys and stuff like that – 'cos when I was coming up they had it sewn up, they was the label of the South, [Geto Boys' label] Rap-A-Lot. I learned rappin' with New York music and then I guess I started to respect it when I heard cats where I'm from, talkin' how I talked."

Unfortunately, the attention wasn't reciprocated: It seemed that the East Coast wasn't trying to hear about hip-hop from down South, even songs that might have been closer in feel to New York than 2 Live Crew's bass songs. Thankfully, Memphis was unique in that it had its own thriving hip-hop scene by the late 1980s, with the radio and mixtape mavericks like DJ Spanish Fly supporting local acts such as Gangsta Pat, SMK and Pretty Tony.

"We always spoke on the prejudices that the East Coast definitely had," says 8Ball, who cites these locals as strong influences in his own work. "It used to be like, if you wasn't from New York as far as hip-hop then you really couldn't go up there and play your music. That's what we spoke on a lot. A lot of the mass media in hip-hop back in the day, if you wasn't from New York or LA you wouldn't get a lot of play. I think folks like the Geto Boys definitely kicked that door open as far as getting respect from both coasts."

8Ball and MJG are children of the blues and soothing soul, while the Geto Boys were weaned on George Clinton's intergalactic P-Funk. As time progresses, a younger generation of rappers now looks to these rap groups, as well as folks like OutKast and Goodie Mob, as their rock-solid foundation. That's not to say there's a thorough dismissal of earlier music – on the contrary, if the rapper has managed to hook up with a producer who loves digging in the crates for old sounds. But, for some, the influence rests squarely on the shoulders of rap from the late 1980s and 1990s.

The streets love 8Ball and MJG for their smart and laid-back pimp flow, and so does a growing sector of the mainstream, which has helped them achieve several gold and platinum honors. Their new fans are growing exponentially, winning folks who may have learned about the duo from the mega-successful Dirty South artists and sometime collaborators Ludacris (who proclaims them his favorites) and OutKast (who consistently show love) or even through their most recent signing to Sean 'P. Diddy' Combs' Bad Boy Records in New York. Their toil has made it easier for newer artists coming into the game to reap the rewards, and while they're the same or similar age to many others in the game, 8Ball and MJG have been elevated to a position of wise elders.

"It's just a blessing," says MJG of Ludacris and OutKast. "The same spirit, the same vibe that was in us when we was doing what we was doing to make them feel the shit that we was saying back then is in them now and they just ridin' it on out. I guess when they give homage and stuff I guess they can feel it. It's just like a musical feeling. All I can do is tip my hat off to them cats and tell them, 'Full speed ahead.'"

> **'back in the day, if you wasn't from new york or la, you wouldn't get a lot of play'**

"Atlanta is hot as a firecracker right now," says multi-platinum rapper Too $hort (Todd Shaw), a part-time resident of the city for more than a decade who has witnessed its grooming into the new Mecca of black music. "Atlanta is making hits. Not just music in studios and the music scene, but motherfucking hit records are coming out of here.

"And I would say something else, 'cos Atlanta is really in love with Atlanta, but I do want to say that I think a large part of Atlanta's success is because so many people from the Midwest migrated to Atlanta to make music. So many people from New York migrated to Atlanta. You got tons of people from Texas, Louisiana, California.

"I mean, they're out here and you're getting certain records that you're going, 'That's Atlanta, that's crunk,' but I'm thinking and knowing that a lot of the stuff that's coming out of Atlanta is a combined effort from the locals and the people they work with. All the different little music crews and then everybody's got a studio, everybody's got their crew, their name, their clique and it ain't just, 'We all born and raised right here in Atlanta.' A lot of the musicians come up out of Chicago and Detroit. A lot of producers down here, they originated from New York and they been down here 10, 12 years."

Of course, the South doesn't exist in its own bubble, and its hip-hop has certainly been influenced by more than music from the region. In particular, the South seems to

Too $hort: "Atlanta is hot as a firecracker right now."

have just as much affection for the smooth soul brothers of Chicago like Curtis Mayfield and Earth, Wind and Fire as for the intergalactic electronic funk of Detroit's P-Funk (helmed by the colorful bandleader George Clinton).

When it comes to hip-hop, the South has always held a natural affinity with the West Coast. Pioneers like $hort, N.W.A, Ice T and Snoop Dogg (who enjoyed a career boost after spending a few years learning business in Louisiana from Master P) earned respect in the South for their honest and raw delivery and unique wordplay – not to mention their hazily blunted beats and roomy basslines, perfect for riding in the car, something not so common in New York, dependent as it is on public transportation.

Albums like Dr. Dre's seminal *The Chronic* (1992) demanded respect on the East Coast, but the praise was not exactly spoon-fed to the West Coast.

"Right now, New York is saying, 'Oh OutKast respect, Too $hort respect, Scarface respect, Luke Skyywalker we respect you,'" says $hort. "But when we were actually coming out for the first time they weren't checking for us. They didn't even wanna hear that shit. Everybody on South's dick [now]. Everybody like, oh, sucking South's dick. It was well deserved though. It was earned. When the South wasn't really getting that respect, they were doing they own thing."

There was another rising star in the West Coast that was resonating in the South, but it took a tragedy to make people realize just how much.

"When Tupac died, nigga, that was like the heartbeat of the South," $hort explains. "[When] Tupac died – that gave everybody a reason to just be like, 'Fuck it!'"

Tupac Shakur was also an honorary ATLien who moved his mother and sister to the Atlanta area in the years before his death in 1996. His mother, Afeni, is currently building the Tupac Amaru Shakur Foundation and Center for the Arts in neighboring Stone Mountain, Georgia. The young revolutionary mind was shaped by many well-documented influences from Huey Newton to Malcolm X to Bob Marley – and the Dirty South's own king, Scarface.

"I used to be at the club and the DJ would put on records off *Makaveli* because *Makaveli* came out right after 'Pac died," remembers $hort. "They would put on records from *Makaveli*, you would swear that nigga was on stage! The whole damn crowd be singing every word. It would be like a concert, and he ain't even there. I just saw how much of an influence Tupac had on Master P and No Limit, how much of an influence Tupac had on the whole city of Atlanta, Georgia, and on Houston, Texas, and just how much influence on that whole 'Bankhead [Bounce]' and getting crunk certain songs of *Makaveli* had on that shit.

"Tupac was so much crunk – his shit was so crunk as far as what crunk meant, you know what I'm saying? He was a part of it even though he had just passed away. But he was a part of it. The Makaveli album was *in it*. It was in the scene." Born out of countless influences and spawning multiple styles, the Dirty South has captured the popular imagination with astute blends of partying, knowledge and pure funk. Detractors might warn that it's got 15 minutes of fame and they're quickly ticking away. But true fans and purveyors of the culture know how much hard work it took to be in this position and know it's going to take an awful lot of muscle to knock the South back down. And that's muscle no one seems to have – for now at least.

"I think every area, every region has the opportunity to be influential in the music industry," reckons Too $hort. "Look at St. Louis. I mean, one guy makes it and it shines the light on all the guys. You got J-Kwon and Chingy and whoever the fuck else just because one dude made it. How many people you think got jobs and food because of all the people I just named? It's a lot of mouths fed just because Nelly made a hit record."

"So that's what David Banner is to Mississippi, that's what Too $hort has been to Oakland … I was up in Indianapolis a couple weeks ago and them muhfuckers are so hungry they ready to hurt somebody to let them in the music industry. They ready to commit violent acts for somebody to let them up in the game. I'm serious. Indianapolis – they were so serious!"

Like anyone serious, prospective players are studying the game, identifying the major winners and analyzing their strategies.

"And the shit that they were playing for me was all South," says $hort. "They like, 'Fuck it, we going with *that* sound.'"

BLACK WALL STREET

FEATURING **Lil Jon, E-40, Ludacris, Bone Crusher and Jazze Pha**

"I really love when people doubt me," says Lil Jon (Jonathan Smith), pointing this out like it's a delicious challenge he's ready to attack with a knife and fork. "Just when they thought I couldn't do R&B, I give Usher the biggest record of his career and the biggest debut in history of R&B for anybody. I'm just doing my job though. I don't really even like to talk about, 'I did this and I did that.' It's about your last hit and how many hits you got. Yeah, [Usher's hit] 'Yeah!' did its thing and whatever, but I need another 'Yeah!' I wanna have 10 of those. Or 15 or 20."

The Atlanta-based DJ/producer has enjoyed several back-to-back pop hits in America in the past two years, but Lil Jon seems like he'd be satisfied with nothing less than the *Guinness* record for all-time chart success. Not that his ego needs the glory; rather, the studio nerd side of him craves the quiet spotlight.

Lil Jon has been a local celebrity in Atlanta for many years, ruling dancefloors with his bombastic club hits. But it's nothing compared to the national attention he started receiving in 2004 as comedian Dave Chappelle began to parody him on his television show, making famous the exclamations Lil Jon calls out on his boisterous party records: *Yeeeaaah! What?!? Okaaaay!*

Chappelle painted a portrait of a smiley, dreadlocked Rasta with a three-word vocabulary. America ate it up. "Shit changed when the Dave Chappelle stuff really hit," he says. "That's when 55-year-old white people started coming up to me knowing who I am. That's when it changed. [Now] I can't really go nowhere without somebody recognizing me. People 'What?' and 'Yeah!' my ass to death but I don't get tired of it. I'm thankful for it."

People who have just learned about Lil Jon in the past few years might be surprised to know that not only does he have more than a one-handed vocabulary, but he's one of the most astute businessmen to sweep through the music industry in a while.

In 2004, he signed a distribution contract for his record label BME (Black Market Enterprises) with industry juggernaut Warner Brothers. For close to a decade preceding the deal, Warner Brothers had relieved itself of nearly all of its black music resources, and by the time Lil Jon signed on, they were intent on giving BME a full push. Meanwhile, his deal with large independent TVT Records for his Lil Jon & The East Side Boyz project and several young artists has resulted in a multi-platinum relationship with the label.

Since the advent of the Dave Chappelle publicity, Lil Jon has learned to work it in front of the camera as well as the boardroom. He moved lightning-quick to build on the brand identity that Chappelle had rocket-launched for him, producing his own energy drink (CRUNK!!!, named after the energetic lifestyle and musical form he's associated with), Oakley sunglasses that play tunes in your ear, T-shirts and even, it is rumored, a couple of action figures. He also hit the media circuit with a vengeance, hosting red carpet proceedings at the MTV Movie Awards with Paris Hilton and providing commentary to VH1's humorous weekly wrap-up show, *Best Week Ever*.

After dozens of television appearances on MTV, VH1 and BET all throughout 2004, Lil Jon has emerged as a self-assured entertainer. He could have a legitimate shot at a career doing comedy films and the like if he were to choose that avenue. Instead, for the time being, he's chosen to start releasing his own adult DVDs, taking cues from Luther Campbell and Snoop Dogg, who have seen much success from that endeavor. Lil Jon's debut foray, *American Sex Series*, was a top-selling urban title in 2004. Even on *ASS* he is a funny and personable guy (though he doesn't, how shall we say, 'mingle' with the porn stars).

"The thing about entertainers today, we're smart," he says. "Once we get in the public eye we know how to make money off ourselves. When you get hot you gotta milk

Lil Jon: Artist, producer and astute businessman.

it 'cos you can't stay hot forever. So I'm trying to do as much work as possible, do as many tracks as possible and hopefully keep my shit going another couple years. So I'm just working hard right now while I'm in the spotlight. I'll take time off later. You sleep when you die."

independent hustle

E-40 (Earl Stevens Jr.) is an innovative West Coast legend who has had an indelible influence on the South, just like his friend and colleague Too $hort. E-40's roots are all in the South, with family in Texas and Louisiana. He studied art at Grambling State University in Louisiana, and although he returned to the San Francisco Bay Area after one year, his work with and appeal within the region has remained steadfast.

Too $hort's music circulated in the Bay Area from the early 1980s on, and E-40 credits $hort as a big part of the reason he exists as an artist at all. Indeed the two are informed by the same 'player' lifestyle, speaking directly to the streets. But where Too $hort tells his pimped-out stories with wry punch, focusing fairly hard on females, E-40 flexes an innovative vocabulary (see Glossary), a delivery style that finds him leaping from rapid-fire verbal bullets to more languid word drops and an imagination that ranges over everything from the late 1980s drought in Northern California to a woozy night on the town.

> 'being with lil jon and the whole new machine, the whole new label, it just revives me'

Too $hort and E-40 have impacted artists and labels in the South with their lyrics and beats as well as the strength of their independent hustle. It is a blueprint that many in the South have adopted to resounding success.

"Selling tapes out the trunk of the car, that was pretty much patented by E-40, Too $hort, Tony Draper at Suave House, Rap-A-Lot, people like that," says E-40. "Then came along the Master Ps of the world and the Cash Moneys. They watched the game and did what they supposed to do and now they reaching for the stars. Ain't no limit, like Master P says … [Cash Money's] Baby and them said, 'Man, we seen y'all for years. We studied y'all for years.' They seen how a muhfucker did it.

"In the early '90s, from '91 or '92, I was always in the South. Up in Houston with [rapper] Mean Green and them in Dallas, with [DJ] Greg Street [in Atlanta], down in Shreveport with [rapper] Jabberjaw. These were the people that help built my career. The West and the South have always been cool. It ain't like just 'cos the South's hot we fucking with 'em. We always fucked with the South. I got platinum and gold records –

I'm on two platinum albums that 8Ball & MJG got. I'm on Master P's album [*I'm Bout It*]. But I been down with these cats even before that though."

After 10 years and 10 albums with Jive Records, the label that's home to Too $hort as well as mainstream pop acts Britney Spears and Justin Timberlake, E-40 has signed to Lil Jon's BME label, distributed by Warner Brothers. Lil Jon is executive producing E-40's new album, *My Getto Report Card*.

"It's not no gimmick, it has nothing to do with me trying to spark some controversy to sell records," he asserts. "It's a definite eye opener for me to sign with BME/Warner, with Lil Jon's label. But at the same time, we got at each other. I talk to him at least once or twice a week and so I had got at him and my deal was up. [I told him], 'I'm outta my contract so what's happenin' with your situation?' So he came with it … My mama always told me wherever I go to show up and show out. That's what's happening. That's what you got to do."

E-40's decision to join Lil Jon at BME was hailed by hip-hop industry pundits as a smart move, positioning him to bring his career to a better platform and opening him up to a far wider audience than he's enjoyed thus far. He will now work with a label boss who knows how to turn a song into a runaway smash and has the energy and the interest to focus on him. It has also sent a strong signal to the New York-centric that the South is a business force that's here to stay.

"With this move that I made with Lil Jon's label, it's really not no shocker," he says. "It fits. It ain't like it's like, 'Oh, that don't seem like that go together. It don't fit in the puzzle.' It don't seem like that 'cos everybody know that I been fucking with the South, period. It ain't like it's some new shit, like, 'Oh, I'm just jumping on the bandwagon 'cos they hot.' It so happened that my contract is up and it's a home for me and he's interested and willing to give it a go and it's like, let's make it unfold.

"[BME artist] Lil Scrappy just went gold, first time artist. That just shows you right there, not only is it talent but you can tell they working the record. They hungry. It's a hungry staff over there. Being with Lil Jon and the whole new machine, the whole new label, it just revives me. It just makes me feel like I'm freshly new again. And it's a blessing to even do something like this.

"I think it's gon' be a monumental album," he predicts, excitement audible in his voice. "I really honestly feel this way."

E-40 and Lil Jon are a winning combination. Soon they will each release what should be the biggest and best records in their respective careers, South and West Coast united in innovative creativity and platinum-coated goals.

"I'm really wondering when are the rap fans gonna step up and say we don't like screaming chants and crunk beats," says Too $hort, playing devil's advocate. "I don't see it in the near future, but they gonna wake up one day and go, 'We don't like that song anymore.' And if that ever happens, I'll bet you Lil Jon's gonna evolve and survive. A

Ludacris (centre) with Juicy J (left) and DJ Paul (right) of Three 6 Mafia.

lotta muhfuckers might fall out the wayside, but he's gonna survive. I saw him last night. He was doing the same thing he was doing five years ago: Sitting at the studio mixing board, getting money."

expect the unexpected

Ludacris (Chris Bridges) is a multi-platinum rapper with an instantly recognizable voice, a budding actor and a humanitarian with a non-profit organization. He's also a bobble-head doll (hip-hop's first), a mischievous puppet (for the prank phone-call show *Crank Yankers* on cable network Comedy Central) and a foul-mouthed gerbil (in the yet-to-be released animated feature film *Lil' Pimp*). And, clearly, a pretty good businessman, too.

During the course of writing this book, Ludacris comes up again and again when people are praising smart business in the Dirty South. Indeed, he is to be commended for more than his lyrically deft, funky and often hilarious songs. Equally impressive are the many moves he's made in the music industry. He's helped to secure major label deals for artists in his Disturbing Tha Peace crew, uses film soundtracks to release singles as advance promotion for his albums and has made sure his label releases several singles off of each of his records. Yet, there is something that people consistently get wrong about him.

"Since I'm a rapper they go ahead and stereotype me as someone that's going to be late and unprofessional all the time, and that's just not me when it comes to working," he says. "Time is of the essence to me and being on time is so important. I think people get that misunderstood and I hate it when they do that because they stereotype me and put me in a category with people that are late but I'm not that type of person. So when they really get to know me they understand that I'm on time and I'm about my business. And I think it's important, because I hate when people waste my time so I'm damn well not trying to waste anybody else's time."

I ask Ludacris how he manages to be both a good businessman and a creative artist, roles that seem to be mutually exclusive in most cases. After all, the seriousness required to negotiate smart contracts seems pretty different from the wild and playful image he portrays on record.

"There's no process," he says. "It's just like you know how to act around your parents and you know how to act around your friends. You can just switch up modes at any time. If you go in your mother's house you know not to curse and then you go outside and just be cursin' up a storm outside and actin' a fool. I don't think it's hard for me to switch from business to creative because it's just different walks of life and you have to know how to act in different situations and how to adjust and definitely know what's what. And I think I'm pretty good at that. So it's not hard at all."

I also want to know his basic business strategy as he moves into the future.

"Expect the unexpected and know that I'm definitely trying to venture out. It's all about cross promotion and whatever we can do, because the smart thing to do is use the Ludacris the name and what people love about me and try different things besides just rapping. Because if people buy into me as an artist, they'll more than likely support me in other areas."

Ludacris just dropped his next album, *Red Light District*. Scope there for a co-branded line of vibrators and sex toys?

bone crusher

"We've got it right now," Bone Crusher (Wayne Hardnett) says of the South's well-earned success in business. "So while you've got it you've gotta make sure and hold on to it for a while. We had been in the gutter so long, was on the streets so long doing it, that by the time there was a deal, we was already ready. A lot of guys don't be ready, they just make a record, it blow up and they're like, 'Damn, what are we gonna do now?'"

Bone's not one of those guys caught out there without a raincoat or a game plan. Instead, as he readies the release of his second album, *Fight Music*, he's also working on several different business plans. He is strategizing the launch of his own brand of Aqua Vigor water, coming up with concepts for a clothing line, working with his wife on her film production company and laying out plans with his own record label, Vainglorious.

> 'if people buy into me as an artist, they'll more than likely support me in other areas'

From Adamsville, on the west side of Atlanta, Bone was able to witness and be inspired by Atlanta's rise to power in the music industry. In the late 1980s and early 1990s, record labels like LaFace, Caper Records and So So Def (Jermaine Dupri's label, with which Bone Crusher would later sign) were introducing the flavor of the city to the rest of the country and the world.

"Growing up in that was crazy for me," he says. "It definitely give you that little edge to be like, whenever times get like, damn, ain't shit gonna happen … you could just look at people that made it and be like, well shit, that muhfucker did it, I can do it too."

Even more than to his debut album *Attenchun!*, Bone's coveted spot in the rap game right now is owed to his memorable breakout smash hit, 'Never Scared,' which was originally a single independently released on Break 'Em Off Records.

"I knew it was gonna be bigger than life but …" he trails off, knowing that at this point it's a bit of an understatement. Despite certain naysayers, "Never Scared" was one of those rare songs that transcends not only regions and occasions but musical genres. It also provided the title for comedian Chris Rock's HBO special and tour in 2003.

"'Never Scared' was a song, it wasn't like it was just a crunk record," says Bone. "It

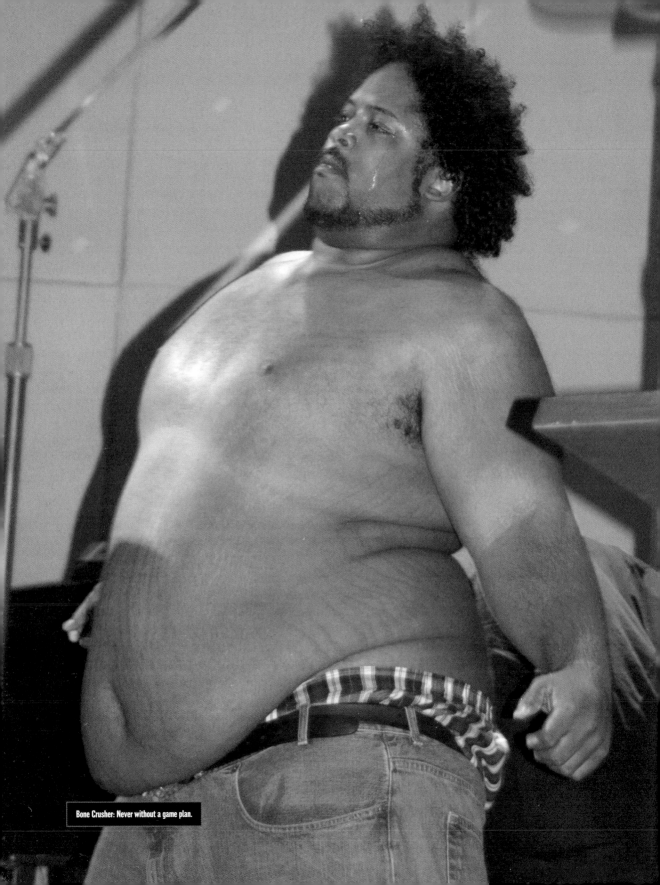

Bone Crusher: Never without a game plan.

had more to it. There was something else about it. People hear it, they were like, 'Damn, that shit's crazy!'"

After blowing up in the Atlanta underground in early 2003, the song turned into a certified smash during the weekend of the city's annual All-Star football game.

"When everybody came down [to Atlanta], that was the first thing they'd say, 'What's the hot shit? What's the hot shit?' It was like yo, this record right here, it was 'Never Scared' and [David Banner's] 'Like a Pimp.' That really took it out. Everybody really took it from the All-Star game that year and took it wherever where they was from and next thing I knew we had 3-4,000 spins [on radio] and it was crazy."

Bone Crusher, shrewd businessman that he is, knew he was sitting on gold. And, again, he had a game plan ready by the time he had a hit. "When JD [Jermaine Dupri] heard it, he was like, 'Man, I've gotta have it. Bone, what you want?' I told him, 'Back the dump truck up with the money.'"

jazze pha

As we see, there's a multitude of business opportunities available to smart representatives of the Dirty South, limited only by their imaginations and the desire to build a strong brand. But while bobble heads, beverages and pornos can add up to big dollars, there are still some who keep their focus on the music and still do very well financially.

Jazze Pha (Phalon Alexander) came out of the womb pre-wired for musical genius, which is probably why everyone and their mother wants him to produce their record. It's also why he's already worked with a very large list of folks, from Busta Rhymes and Bobby Womack to Aaliyah and Tupac, though he still looks forward to the day when he can add Quincy Jones, Prince and Patti LaBelle to that resumé.

Considering his achievements so far, one of those collaborations is probably not that far off.

His mother, Deniece Williams, is an accomplished singer who's worked with Stevie Wonder and Barbra Streisand among others, while dad James Alexander, the legendary bassist with the Bar-Kays, has played on albums from people like Isaac Hayes, the Staple Singers and Albert King.

Growing up, Jazze remembers being around a lot of rock stars infatuated with funk and R&B due to his parents' jobs.

"I was around Mick Jagger. He was really fascinated with my dad's group," he recalls. "He used to show up in the pit and take in the performance. Just really studying the whole movement. And then, even like when I've seen him doing stuff, when they did a big tour and they did 'Start Me Up,' it was certain things that the lead singer in my dad's group was doing, he was doing.

"Certain moves that he was doing on stage were really taken from there. Just like

Jazze Pha: "You gotta have a great big menu."

Michael Jackson might get something from Fred Astaire or Sammy Davis. It's just passed on, you know?"

Jazze lived in California with his mom and, if he did well in school during the year, would get to go on tour with his dad (who lived in Memphis) over the summer.

"That was like the highlight of my life," he told Atlanta weekly newspaper *Creative Loafing*, recalling summers touring with the Bar-Kays as they played with artists like George Clinton and Rick James.

No one would dispute that his funk/soul lineage is fairly well intact. Jazze's musical prowess is likely a combination of genetics and a blessing from God. There are times when he feels an unseen force at work in the studio. "Sometimes you black out and you do something and everybody in the control room is goin' crazy and the feeling is just there," he says. "Something is coming through you and it's just soul. You can't predict it, you can't tell it where to go, it just comes."

A confessed people person, Jazze is in touch with all musical walks of life, from rappers and R&B singers to gospel greats, which allows him to have a very well-balanced repertoire. "It's like when you're a chef or a caterer and you doing an event. Sometimes you might be doing a soul picnic for an urban radio station and then on the other hand you might be doing something for some white-collar business people and you wanna serve up a whole kind of different dish. You gotta have a great big menu.

> **"Something is coming through you and it's just soul – you can't predict it"**

"I don't call myself a South beat maker. I make beats that sound like the South but sometimes I make things and people have no idea," he says, citing songs he's produced for people like Slick Rick and P. Diddy that most people don't associate with him.

Soon, he's back to the food analogy to describe his tasty morsels of music. He says he's got more spices in his pantry than most give him credit for. "It's kinda like when you go to Roscoe's Chicken and Waffles in Los Angeles," he says. "You want those special waffles or those chicken wings. So I gotta give 'em some of those ingredients, but then people don't know that they got these great potatoes too, you know what I'm saying? I try to give them a little variety."

It's hard to find a major album coming out of the South without a Jazze Pha production on it, not to mention the healthy amount of work he does outside of the region, so he must have an insanely devoted work ethic. I ask him what a typical day entails.

"Most of the time I wake up, handle a lotta phone calls in the day time. Probably around 4pm I get with my son, spend a little time with my son, might take him out to eat or something like that and probably 6:30 I'm in the studio working every day on everybody, whatever I'm doing. I'm there 'til four or five in the morning.

"I work so well on my own and I got a team that works so well with me, I can put somebody in a little room and do a record for Ruben Studdard in 45 minutes and have another writer go do it somewhere else. So we gettin' records done."

This all sounds a bit Motown to me. I tell him it sounds like, to put it in possibly unfortunate terms, a hit factory. After all, he is celebrating the number one success of Ciara, the R&B singer who is his first artist on his Sho'Nuff label, and is preparing to bring out two more young artists, Young Geezy and Jody Breeze, as well as his own debut album *Big Luv*.

"'Hit factory,' that's a great phrase!" he exclaims. "I like that phrase! I mean, that's what I'm doing. I made a track right before I came from home "cos I got a little set-up at home where I can make music. I mp3'd it to Los Angeles and then my partner called me as I was on my way to work. When I got to work he had a song that was just great. And I'm like okay, what if I hadn't sent that? You know, and that's a song that I guarantee somebody's gonna buy by the end of this weekend. I'll have the song tonight by probably 9 o'clock. When I get out of here at about 3am I'll have two songs done, two brand new songs from zero with guitars played, horns, pianos, organs – everything."

Like Lil Jon, Jazze Pha doesn't seem like he makes sleep so much of a priority, either. "My mom and all of them, they be on my back about that kinda stuff because you gotta get your rest and it's important," he says. "But you can't stop the motive."

ANATOMY OF A HIT

FEATURING **Too \$hort, Lil Jon & The East Side Boyz, Ying Yang Twins and I-20**

To sniff out whether or not an artist or song is a potential hit, most traditional major label record companies rely on what they call their director of A&R (which stands for "artists and repertoire"). The A&R director is responsible for finding, signing and developing artists throughout their career with the label.

A&R has always been a coveted job. One reason is the ego-stroking satisfaction that comes when decisions are made based on your say. The other is the lifestyle it affords, even for those that aren't technically top earners.

Although there are notable exceptions, the A&R is traditionally seen as a sort of smug, middle-aged white guy. He sits with his feet kicked up on a glass conference table in the high-rise office of his New York or Los Angeles-based record label, poised to dictate what's cool. And he feels like an even bigger bad-ass after having survived 15 years of corporate lay-offs with his cocaine and lap dancing expense account intact.

What we might not always think of when it comes to A&R is how the record company guy gets his information in the first place. After all, Bill from the Big Apple high-rise on the Avenue of the Americas is not going to be hanging down on the corner of Martin Luther King in New Orleans to find the hottest young rapper. Chances are, he's not even trying to head uptown from his comfortable midtown Manhattan perch to find local Harlem or Bronx-based talent.

One of the A&R director's most important assets in the hip-hop world is the DJ. These days they're paying acute attention not only to club play but also to the growing mixtape sector.

"DJs work hand in hand with A&Rs and mix show directors," explains DJ Smallz, an influential club, mixtape and Sirius Satellite Radio DJ from Florida. "[A&R directors] get my mixtapes too and they see who's really popping and then they bring them in for showcases. It's a whole system."

"DJs are at least street A&Rs," he says, "'cos we're listening to more of the street music. The A&R takes it and brings it to who they got to bring it to and then they soften the image up and make it more commercialized. But we take the raw stuff and kinda feed it to 'em, who's really hot in this market. 'Cos they can't be everywhere, you know what I mean? So we're kind of an extension of that, and we get paid through the mixtapes. That's kind of like our A&R payment."

Smallz puts out a new mixtape – all in CD format these days, despite the name – approximately every three weeks. And while his sets are largely comprised of exclusives and already established hits from big artists, he also uses the mixtapes as a forum to be a talent scout for these A&R directors and introduce them to someone he feels might be of the same caliber as the stars.

"Mixtapes are really influential to break the music out," he emphasizes. "Because you're using the big guys like Lil Jon on your CD to showcase some of the underground talent, people are obviously getting your CD not just to hear the newest music but to hear the big stars. So you kinda do some psychological shit and get them to listen to underground stuff. A little bit of underground, you know what I mean? You slip it in where you can. My tapes are probably 75-80 per cent commercial artists but maybe 15-20 per cent underground: I just try to slip it in there. And then when people see that name so many times – like Chamillionaire, they see Chamillionaire on my track list every time I drop – they know that it's a major artist, just not signed yet."

Interestingly enough, Texas's Chamillionaire signed a deal with major label Universal Records shortly before our interview.

One former A&R director who always defied the stereotypical form and formula is

Lil Jon, who once worked for Jermaine Dupri's So So Def label in Atlanta. Then, as now, Jon is a DJ first and foremost; it's the groundwork for everything he does. He no longer plays that role but, as he explains, he likes to 'A&R' all his records before submitting them to anyone else. Even that goes right back to DJing.

"I think really what it is, when I make records I think how a DJ thinks: In breaks," he says. "A real DJ thinks when he mixes, he mixes where the breaks are 'cos when you hit the breaks, that's the hottest part of the record and that's the part that the crowd sings and that's the part that takes the party to the next level. So when I make records I make them in breaks. Like when you listen to 'Damn,' [his instrumental for YoungBloodZ] it starts off with no 808 [drum machine]. Then when the 808 comes in it makes you go crazy. Then it goes from the verse to the chorus and it takes you up a whole 'nother notch."

Constructed with synthesizers, turntables and drum machines, Lil Jon records tend to spotlight deep and heavy bass and with spare melodies, perfect cocoons for the rowdy chants that punctuate crisp and clean beats.

His songs typically have what Too $hort calls "the fight sequence" portion of the song, where the tune stops and quickly switches gears into a bigger sound. This is the part where people lose their minds on the dancefloor (or in the car, house, etc.). His DJ training enables him to place the fight sequence in just the right place to capitalize on a maximum energy surge.

"When I'm in the studio mixing the records I'm thinking about what the crowd is gonna do on this part and that part and this part. I take myself out of me and I become the crowd. I close my eyes and let the music take me somewhere. If it don't move me right, I change the break up. I totally become the crowd. That's why the records make people do what they do because … I'm the crowd."

"I don't care what none of you say/There is not a better way/To make your pay in the USA …"
YING YANG TWINS, 'Pink Panther'

Atlanta in particular features yet another type of underground A&R, one with the surprising power to detect hits like a heat-seeking missile hurtling towards its target. Which, in some cases, turns out to be the top of the *Billboard* pop charts.

This A&R doesn't work in a high-rise office building. And, most of the time at least, she doesn't rock the crossfader or the turntables. She takes her clothes off for a living.

"Out here in Atlanta, you always had those records that didn't come from the radio, they didn't come from the club where everybody goes out to dance," says Too $hort. "They didn't come from just the streets where somebody was like, 'This is an underground hit.' The record came straight out of the strip club. They were records that

Club class: Lil Jon still thinks like a DJ.

you probably only heard in strip clubs for weeks and months before they would cross over to a dance club or get picked up by a radio station. And a lot of records broke in Atlanta through strip clubs, you know?"

"I got this one homeboy in Atlanta, every time I do a record I take it to him and let him play it. He works at a strip club," says Lil Jon. "Strippers are always the best judges of what's gonna be the shit or not because they dance to music every day all day. So I always take him the records."

Lil Bo (Wendell Neal) and Big Sam (Sam Norris) are Lil Jon's multi-platinum partners-in-crunk, better known as rowdy chanters The East Side Boyz. They agree that the strip clubs in Atlanta are the first and most honest testing ground for their records.

"We take all our music to the strip clubs just to see how the girls gon' react to it, how good they dance," says Lil Bo. "So eventually it's become a big tradition for us to go to the strip clubs. People that's in the strip club, if they keep hearing your music at the strip club they eventually gon' get it."

Lil Bo pauses to explain that, in Atlanta, a lot of people don't go to the regular nightclubs, preferring the strip clubs instead. "A lot of people just go to the strip club because it's more relaxed. You get to see women, you ain't gotta worry about nobody fighting or when rowdy music come on you ain't gotta worry about nobody pushin' nobody, just lay back, know what I'm saying? And then there's so many of them so it isn't like you're going to the same one every night."

"Just in the local area of Atlanta we've got like 58 strip clubs," confirms I-20, of Ludacris' Disturbing Tha Peace crew. "So if you're not big in the strip clubs, don't even waste your time."

"You go into our strip clubs and you see men and women, couples, married couples, guy mighta just met the girl down the street or whatever," says Big Sam. "And you go in there and it's really like being a regular club but it's just girls dancing and getting naked and all that type stuff. You gonna have you a good time because the DJ is gonna play all the hottest stuff that's at the clubs right now. So it's like being away from the normal club environment as far as worrying about getting hit in the head with a bottle when a Lil Jon and The East Side Boyz record come on."

Lil Bo paints a picture of a thriving social scene perpetuated by the strip clubs, particularly the ones in the hoods of Atlanta. Between them there are amateur nights and kickboxing tournaments with large cash prizes as well as musical talent nights for hopeful rappers. When they have a record to try out, it will make the rounds on a certain circuit. "We'll take it to Blue Flame. We'll take it to Pin Up. We'll take it to Stroker's. We'll take it to Jazzy T's. All the hood booty clubs."

I ask him if there's a certain club where the strippers are harder to impress. One that perhaps has a streak of elitist music critic running up in it. "Blue Flame would be like that," he replies. "The Blue Flame, they're more like uppity type women. If it jumps off in there, that let you know you got yourself a *song*, you know what I'm saying? So that's pretty cool."

Lil Jon and the East Side Boyz hit meteoric status with the single 'Get Low,' a song which has enjoyed an extended shelf life in a fleeting pop world as well as several remix incarnations in the underground. The video pays homage to the strip club that gave the song its first inclination of future success, as the group and featured guests Ying Yang Twins take over the Blue Flame. However, the song wasn't an instant success at the Blue Flame.

> 'we take all our music to the strip clubs, just to see how the girls gon' react to it'

"We first started by taking 'Get Low' to the club," remembers Lil Bo. "When they first heard it, a lot of women in the club wasn't really feeling it – like two, three women were dancing. And we went back like a week later, and they played 'Get Low' again, mo' women started getting to it. At the time we was trying to figure out was 'Get Low' gon' be the next single. So we went back like a week after that and finally all the women in the club started jamming to it. And Jon was like, 'Well, okay, that's gon' be the song.' And it went on from there.

"But when we first put it in there they wasn't really feeling it like that, so Jon was kinda like, 'Oh, I don't know if this is the one.' Then we went back, before he was like, 'Naw this not gon' be the one at all, naw this ain't it.' He went back and seen that everybody was dancing to it. Even the people at the bar that don't even work there, they was feelin' it too, so Jon was like, 'Okay this is it then.' It just so happened everybody was bouncing to it and he was like, 'Okay this is it.' I'm glad he went with that song because it was very popular."

Lil Jon doesn't use the strip clubs so much to test the layers of sound in his production as much as to just figure out whether he's pushing the right record.

"I don't really make changes. The only change I might make is the mix might not sound right at the club. I may need to turn the 808 up, turn the kick up."

For Lil Jon, the strip club has also been a place of revelation as far as being attuned to what works in his own sound. "When you make it, people wanna bite your sound and you gotta come again fresh," he says. "So everybody now is trying to find them little synthesizers [the Novation Polyphonic Synth module], when it's all dance sounds. I thought about it one day when I was in a strip club, and I was in a strip club that don't play no rap. Every techno song that came on had the same sounds that I use on my records. I'm like, that's why my shit is working too is because it's basically hip-hop dance music, you know what I'm saying?"

"This lady said one time that we had voodoo in our music," says Big Sam. "Like every time our music come on no matter what you doing it makes you move. No matter what kind of mood you in it makes you move. And I started watching people's reactions when we played a song they ain't even heard yet. Soon as the music start like they body just start moving. Heads just start bobbing. Like they can't help themselves."

Road testing songs in the Atlanta strip clubs has become a way of life for a number of artists, labels and producers big and small. "The girls' butts don't lie," says Michael 'Taz' Williams of Florida's Dirty Down Records on the brilliant documentary *Dirty States of America*. "If the girls' butts move to a record, I got a *record*."

"I test all my records in the strip club," affirms Jermaine Dupri, talking to Atlanta's *Creative Loafing*. "I feel like that's the place where you can get the most spins on your records, anyway – in the strip club. If the girls really like to dance off one of your records, nine times out of ten, it's gon' be a hit record."

In the same story, Atlanta-based independent artist Al Biggz expresses the same opinion to writer Ronda Racha Penrice. His thoughts are rather more forthright and illustrative to the reader than those of Dupri, and address a more immediate sales potential.

"I look at it as an experience," reasons Biggz. "You know how many niggas that it's their first time being in a strip club? So, nigga, if Al Biggz is playing the first time, she is putting those titties in my face, that song is going to stay with me. That's how I look at it. Those nights be memorable nights for motherfuckers, *historical* nights for motherfuckers."

> '**if the girls really dance off your record, nine times out of ten, it's gon' be a hit**'

"I'm from a city where a stripper's always been a star," says I-20. "Because there's so many strip clubs. Stripping in Atlanta is the girls' equivalent to drug dealing, and it's always been that. I never been nowhere else in the world where I seen like here, where a stripper got a Benz, she got her own VIP section in the club, she's known by name.

"The strip club is huge," he continues. "The stripper is your first test audience if you're a local rapper. And whatever she keeps requesting to dance off of, that's gonna be the shit and that's what's gon' leak it to the regular club and that club's gon' leak it to the radio. It's no different than going to a regular club or concert and you are sitting down with your girls till your record come on. You wait until that one record you love come on and you go, 'Ahh that's my shit!' And you go to the dancefloor and dance for that song and then go sit your ass right back down. It's the same thing in the strip club.

"How it works in Atlanta is somebody records a record, then it goes to the strip club and it becomes the stripper's anthem first. And then, when it becomes her anthem, every

46

nigga in the club want the DJ to play it 'cos if you gon' spend your $10 you want the girl to be into it. So you hope that you record the record that the girls are into, okay? And then it becomes the strip club anthem, period, because the patrons in the strip club, now they crunk off it. To the point that it goes to the regular club, and when you go to the regular club, stripper gets off work she also go to the regular club. She wanna hear that record too. That's it, you know what I'm saying? So the DJ then, he becomes amped and wanna play it because everybody's requesting it to the point that – bam! —the radio say, 'Oh shit, we better jump on it.'"

I-20 (who we will hear from a bit more in the chapter entitled "On the Verge") should know. He's seen it happen with 'Break Bread,' the first single off of his debut album *Self-Explanatory*. The song traveled from the hood strip clubs of Atlanta into homes across America via radio play and regular rotation of the video on BET over the course of the summer of 2004.

"It's just now getting to the rest of the world," he says, tracing back the short history of the song two months after its creation. "I recorded this record early June, we gave it to the clubs in late June, so by the time my birthday rolled around on July 8th it was the shit down here. It takes a minute for the rest of the world to catch on and we just did it for the clubs, man, because we know it works. And then we always give it to [Memphis strip club] Premiere too because they always show me a lot of love. So it's the shit in Memphis too. And it's breaking out now. Now we finally went for adds [adding the record to radio playlists], like, four days ago, and you got 70 major urban stations and on the first day I got added to 58. Which is huge because they're all paying attention and they can't deny how the response is back here at home. So nobody wants to seem like they're the radio station that's late.

"With 'Break Bread,' I got the number one most added single in America because it's the stripper anthem down here. Because we're saying, 'Break Bread,' and that's their motto! 'Yeah, muhfucker, spend sumthin'!' I'm immediately seeing the difference in response of how fast this record is taking off because it's the shit in the strip club down here. It's the song down here when everybody's in the club, filled to capacity, one o'clock in the morning. And the DJ lets you know he's gonna play it 'cos he turn the record off and say it before it comes on."

I-20 explains how the record always receives rewinds, a DJ technique where they will encourage crowd participation and build up energy and enthusiasm by stopping the record and starting it over at key points. "That's when you know you got a good record," he says.

The rapper, however, chose to defy the easy route in bringing 'Break Bread' above ground. When it came time to shoot the video, he resisted the notion to film the sort of raw strip club video that airs on BET's barely censored late night video program *UnCut*. Instead, he wrote a treatment for a different kind of video featuring himself with

The Ying Yang Twins broke through with an ode to Atlanta's strippers.

Ludacris and Bone Crusher (his guests on the song) as well as Lil Jon. One main setting in the video has the artists bringing their crazily animated presence to a bright red padded room, insane asylum style.

I-20's label asked him early on in the process of his album if he wanted to make an *UnCut* video, a marketing tool increasingly favored by new and established hip-hop artists alike. "Nah, I told em I was cool," he says, declining their suggestion. He wanted to be more creative, but he doesn't down the show at all. "It's cool because underground is taking back over hip-hop and *UnCut* has made that possible.

"People owe *UnCut* money," he chuckles. "I'mma put it like that. There's a record that probably never woulda got a spin anywhere else but because it was on *UnCut* all of a sudden the rest of the world is giving it a shot. So people owe *UnCut* some money."

"I think what started happening is you got a different vibe from the strip club songs," says Too $hort. "And then they had all these little what you might call hole-in-the-wall clubs. Really small, but they'd be packed in. The kind of clubs where you'd have to go up in the hood to get to the club. The most famous one was the 559 on the west side of Atlanta by the West End Mall. And the 559 became the club that epitomized what is crunk. What is it? Where do you hear it? Where can you see it? It was at the 559."

The now defunct 559 nightclub is the club most credited along with the local strip clubs for breaking Lil Jon and the East Side Boyz' early records. And by the sound of it, it was more than a lively place to be.

"It was the smallest club that was so fucking packed, and all I can say is a fight didn't mean shit in there," Too $hort remembers, marveling at the thought. "Nobody was gonna leave, nobody was gonna run, nobody ducked for cover. It was a fight, it was just it happened, it's over. It was like some crazy shit! And then the fuckin' club was so little that most of the people couldn't even get in the shit. It'd be a club outside. The parking lot, it'd just be 1000 muhfuckers. 559 is right across the street from the West End Mall and people would just ride around the mall, like a sideshow in the Bay Area. People would just ride around and it would just be a traffic jam – it would be the shit."

Too $hort still seems to give the strip clubs more influence when it comes to putting records on a path to success, but notes it is not the only type of place with the power. "I think the strip club is very much a part of it: The drinking, the gold teeth, and, you know, the No Limit Master P songs.

"The strip clubs was very much a part of it but then, these little neighborhood hole-in-the-wall clubs started breaking records too. If a record was jumping at the 559, if the only place you heard it was the 559 and it was a hit in the 559, sure enough it would be a hit on the radio sooner or later. It would be in every club, it would go from a club like the 559 and it would end up in the strip club.

"You started having different avenues of breaking these records and still radio would not be the first one to set it off, the dance club would not be the first one to set it off. It would either come from the strip club or the neighborhood club. And that pretty much made it solid, like certified, that the crunk music is a movement."

$hort moved to Atlanta from Northern California in 1993, and it would be a few years before he would grasp the potential of the hits he could make in the South. Once he saw the light though, there was no turning back.

The multi-platinum artist is currently working on his 16th album, a huge feat for any genre but particularly notable in hip-hop. It's being recorded in Atlanta, with production duties falling mainly to local greats Lil Jon and Jazze Pha (backed with a few tunes from longtime $hort collaborator, California's Ant Banks). Now, working with Dirty South producers is a business no-brainer for him, but in the mid-1990s it wasn't something he looked at quite as seriously.

The turning point came when he collaborated with Lil Jon on a song called 'Couldn't Be a Better Player' in 1998.

"I was a regular at the 559 at that point," $hort remembers. " I didn't used to hang out with Lil Jon. We were on speaking terms. We knew each other. Of course he knew what I did. He worked at So So Def; of course I knew what he did. And Jermaine [Dupri] would be shooting videos and Lil Jon would be at the videos. Before he was a recording artist he was an implant in the Atlanta music scene, known by his name, face recognition, [people] knew he was a producer and knew he was a DJ. He was in there."

> **he's currently working on his 16th album – a huge feat, particularly in hip-hop**

The song wasn't something he necessarily expected would be a hit, so he turned his attention to other things as Lil Jon took the record and started to promote it amongst his usual channels.

"He was probably networking with certain mix DJs at the radio stations and getting them to play Jermaine's stuff and [also] whatever he was in on, him and [partner Emperor] Searcy. So he basically just got that record out there. I was just using the record for a compilation. I put out a double album called *Nationwide Independence Day*. I was just putting the album together; I wasn't really pushing the single or anything. Lil Jon ran with it. He said, 'Give it to me.'

"We got wax pressed up, we shot a video to it with naked girls and stuff. We shot the video at the strip club, The Gentlemen's Club, and partly in my studio. We pressed up maybe 5-10,000 VHS cassettes. We gave out the single, we gave out the video. I wasn't really first hand into the whole process of pushing tapes or handing out the single. I was putting the album together to get it on the street and get it in the record stores.

"He came and got me and said, 'I need you to come to 559 with me.' Now I've never really hung out with him at that point. We knew each other, studio, whatever. I complimented him on his shit, he respected my shit – we already went through all that. He said, 'Come go to the 559 with me. I wanna show you something.' And I figured kind of what he wanted, he wanted me to see how they reacted when 'Couldn't Be a Better Player' came on. But I didn't know that at that point we had slipped in on the hottest record in Atlanta. Like, somebody always got the hottest record in Atlanta. If you got the hottest record in Atlanta you're destined for fame and success, you know? So I'm knowing what he's gonna do, he's gonna wait till the song comes on and he's gonna say, 'Look at the crowd!' I already knew what it was.

"The song comes on. From the first boom boom – it's got a little slow start, the 808 kicks in before any vocals – and they fuckin' just reacted off the first boom. So I get a little chills, a little goose bumps, and I'm like, 'Yeah I feel ya.' And the beat kicks in and they fuckin' go crazy, the crowd's in a frenzy. Remember I told you if you got a 559 hit, things are gonna happen. So we got a hit in the 559 but in all Lil Jon songs you got the breakdown, fight sequence, where the beat changes and it sends the crowd into an extra frenzy. And in this song, that part came. It comes like two, three minutes into the song. So the change is coming and I'm thinking he already showed me what he wanted to show me. And he said, 'Now this is what I came to show you, watch this.' The fucking change came, them muhfuckers – you know, you gotta ask him – all I know is, shit went crazy. The muhfuckers went crazy outta their fucking heads. And right there it just clicked that I need to be connected with this dude, need to get some more of this. I'm like, this dude is a megastar – and I know him!"

Two other Atlanta megastars that come to mind these days when thinking about strip club-generated hits are the Ying Yang Twins. "We on something else other than the whole Atlanta rap scene," proclaims Kaine (Eric Ron Jackson Jr.) from the back of a limo careening through Hollywood. "We on something else. *Ow ow owwwwwww!*" He howls like a wolf.

His 'brother' D-Roc (D'Angelo Holmes) punctuates that notion with his trademark sound, "Hanh!" It's kind of like a mutation of Lil Jon's famed exclamations.

"The strip clubs been popping since me and my brother were about five years old," says Kaine. "Atlanta got put on the map through Ice Cube. He said we had the best strip clubs in the world. That was a long, long, long, long, long, long, long time ago."

An even longer time ago, Luke and 2 Live Crew were shouting out Atlanta strip clubs like Magic City from down in Miami, and pioneers of Atlanta bass like DJ Smurf were incubating their records in strip clubs. Now DJ Smurf is known as Beat-In-Azz (though everyone seems to unofficially still call him Smurf). With the help of his brother (his actual brother, Derrick Crooms), he is the Ying Yang Twins' manager, and has produced several tracks for them. It was his idea for the group to hone in on the strip clubs.

"When we first started dealing with him we had our talent, but his first words were,

Beat-In-Azz, formerly DJ Smurf, manages the Ying Yang Twins. "I'm selling sex," he told them.

-TOWN.

'I'm selling sex,'" Kaine recalls. "So shit, I mean everybody that can plainly think about sex, they may have a problem trying to express it. 'cos everybody wanna experience it before they go, unless they scared. Yeah but we ain't never scared," he laughs.

The Ying Yang Twins formed in 1998 and broke out into national attention in 2000 with 'Whistle While You Twurk,' an ode to strippers which got slapped for copyright infringement by the owner of the song 'Whistle While You Work' from Disney's *Snow White and the Seven Dwarfs*. The song even name-checks local Atlanta strip clubs like Blue Flame, Stroker's and Magic City. "'Whistle While You Twurk' was our first shot," explains Kaine of the track's early days. " We took 'Whistle While You Twurk' to Magic City."

Playing music at Magic City was DC The Brain Supreme, who scored an infectious pop hit himself with 1995's 'Whoomp! There It Is' by Tag Team.

"DC The Brain Supreme was on the mic, the DJ," says Kaine. "We go up to the booth. Smurf says, 'Spin this for me.' DC The Brain Supreme got up on the mic, he said, 'God damn it, here you go. You gon' hear this for the first time. You might hear it again or God damn it, you might not never hear it no mo.'

"Soon as he dropped the muhfucker – you know how in [Ice Cube's 1998 movie] *The Player's Club* when Bernie Mac hit the green button? Boy, that song, it was just like that! Muhfuckers was just like, 'Gimme that CD! I'll give you $50!' Therefore you know you got a hit when you take it somewhere and all women hit the flo'. They ain't ever trying to stand back and not let you know your shit's jammin', you know what I'm saying? Women gon' come out with it right there at the beginning."

Like Lil Jon & the East Side Boyz, Ying Yang Twins are now accepted on that broader level of popular music. The Twins now have some significant mainstream pop moments on their resume, including guesting on Britney Spears' *In The Zone* album and hosting an episode of the MTV series *Cribs* in which they showed off their own crisp digs.

What started in the strip clubs has now reached that tipping point for the Twins, but Kaine says that now that they have that widespread attention, they intend to display a new side to their work (if maybe in the same context).

"See now how much emphasis is on [sex and strip clubs], I feel like the same emphasis can go toward the everyday surrounding man," he says. "Everybody don't club all they life 'cos shit, you gotta get it. You got to get up and get it. So if you're getting up and getting it you can't be clubbing all the time. See that's the part what makes the Ying Yang music so good for the streets, because you can get up in the morning and pop our CD in and feel like you're at the club. Drink you a cup of coffee, pop in a Ying Yang CD and you'll be up then!

"We doing different types of songs on the next go round," he reveals. "It will be like a more yang approach. For every good, there's bad. So to justify the whole group it has to be a ying period and a yang period. That way at the end people will know who the

Ying Yang Twins are. We ain't represented ourselves on the whole yet. All the like club shit, that's like the ying shit 'cos it consists of you havin' fun and [getting] fucked up and all that. The yang shit is, it's a little bit more disgruntled. It's some everyday problems.

"The same when a song come up out I just wanna give people what they need which is some uplifting route in general man rapping, not so much from man to man or man to women. I wanna speak on behalf of all men and make them say when they hear the song, 'Stuff sho' do be like that. Sho' is.' You know what I'm saying?"

Though Kaine warns of different songs on the way, you probably won't hear anything overly violent during the yang phase of the Ying Yang Twins. "Everybody already promised to die," he says, "so you don't need me just tryin' to die."

Further display of their yin-yang dynamic is in the different audiences they command. It's D-Roc's that's most on display at the moment, and Kaine's that has the potential to widen more.

"It ain't no secret, the females love my brother," Kaine points out. "I click with dudes. I'm more of a street-oriented type dude. I'm more of a street-affiliated cat. That actually comes out in every city we go in. The women be chasing my brother down, boy!"

Ultimately, that's what I call 'girl power,' when the talented female hustlers of the Atlanta booty clubs can have so much A&R power in a male dominated music industry. In the case of the Twins, it's given them the platform to speak out more. They might not abandon the decadent sway of the stripper-crafted song to write hymns or anything, but they strive to expand on their career as more meaningful entertainers.

"Once I put out there what the yang side is about, it's gon' make a lot of people eat words," Kaine insists. "He who laughs last laughs the best. The Ying Yang what you hear on the radio right now, that's like teenage club music. And people don't know that if you want to stay popular you got to stay in the club. And people don't understand that everybody grows up, goes through their phase and gets old. So once they come out of the club, if you tryin' to leave the club with them, you ain't gon' make it. You need to stay in the club."

It's more conscious clubbing, maybe even subliminal crunk. But it's clear that the hard working Twins have more to show us than a mouth full of gold teeth, and there's more to come.

"My brother is the presence of the group and I am the strength, and the world don't know that. They think that what he does is the strength. Actually they like that more. I'm more of a grim character. And if we can put songs together that good on the club tip, what you think my brain clickin' on, on the [other, more serious] side? We have substance, subject matter. We're gon' be talkin' about some weird stuff but that's to get in. See, people like sin better. My brother like 'mo' party.' I'm like 'less party.'

"I see some brain boggling," he forecasts. "I see some ground shaking. Evidence on what I'm speaking to you about now that you ain't even close to hearing yet."

DIVINE INVENTION

FEATURING **Cee-Lo and Chyna Whyte**

"Niggas livin' lawless, niggas labeled hardest/Gonna see whose life is shortest/Regardless this whole world to me is garbage/Tryin' to reap my harvest/I'm starvin' less than a life of ballin'/Yet still tryin' to find my callin' …"
— *CHYNA WHYTE ON 'BIA' BIA' 2 (REMIX)' BY LIL JON & THE EAST SIDE BOYZ*

"Well, I'm a species so rare the human eye's hardly seen/A thin line between divine and killing machine …But to lose my composure I don't normally do/I just thought that you should know/I've been sicker than you … "
— *CEE-LO, 'MEDIEVAL TIMES (GREAT PRETENDER)'*

It's been about four years since Chyna Whyte (Stephanie Martin) was seen brandishing a giant red ax. So there's no need for alarm. The hatchet – a prop for her hard-hitting appearance in the Lil Jon & The East Side Boyz' 'Bia' Bia' 2 (Remix)' video, the hit for which she's best known – has now been buried, both literally and figuratively.

Today Chyna's arms are filled by her baby girl, Christin, who is, alongside her husband, one of her main sources of inspiration and evolution from a hard street life in New Orleans' 9th Ward to her current roles as mama and legal businesswoman.

> "i was lost man – i was out there drinking and smoking and at the club, acting wild"

"My child – she is spoiled, so she just wanna hang on me all day," she says with a weary laugh. "The last few songs I recorded I had to record holding her in my arms. And she is heavy. I was sweatin' and she was sleepin' on my shoulder and I was recording the song and I'm like, 'Yo, I wish somebody could tape this, 'cos this is some real shit right here.' It's some real shit."

Outside of her family, Chyna's guiding force for the last several years has been God. The South is, of course, a devoutly religious stretch of the United States where organized religion is an undeniable force. Chyna says she's always loved God, but did not have an organized foundation growing up.

"For me, I was never raised in the church," Chyna explains. "Never. Never! I'm just tapping into this. God has been keeping his eye on me all my life because I shoulda been

Chyna Whyte: Struggling to embrace a better path.

dead long time ago. I'm talkin' bout *a long time ago*. And he kept me here. It's like, why? I never was in the church. Even though my mama loved God, she never talked to me about God. She never said, 'Stay a virgin, keep yourself, blah blah blah ...'

"All throughout my life, God always put somebody in my life to tell me. Up until right now – because I got saved in 1990-something – I'm not realizing the power of God til right now. So it's a process. But he always kept somebody in my life telling me about Him. So I'm totally different, I'm not the normal holy, you know, go to church [person]. 'Cos a lotta people that go to church, that go to church every Sunday faithfully, don't even have the Holy Spirit. Don't even know what it is to build a relationship with God."

For those people from disadvantaged 'hoods who may have turned to illegal means of getting by at one point or another, reconciling the mentality of a hustler with a strong conviction in God's existence and power is a delicate balancing act. It's an act made ever more tenuous if the person in question happens to be an entertainer in a music genre cloaked in sex, drugs and violence. With a public profile to maintain, that inner struggle is potentially on display.

It's often a battle between the flesh and the soul: A more complicated version of the angels and devils sitting on the shoulders of characters in *Looney Tunes* cartoons. And so it's been for Chyna. By her own admission, Chyna Whyte – whose alias is a play on "china white," meaning cocaine – was once very far from living right. "I was lost, man," she remembers. "I was drinking and smoking and out there wil'ing out at the club. Acting wild. I done went to prison, house arrest, you know, a whole bunch of stuff."

As a result, the subject matter of a lot of her songs reflected those negative influences. And eventually her destructive lifestyle really began to take its toll, both on herself and others. She began to question why she was one of the ones still standing.

"Falling asleep behind the wheel. I coulda died so many times driving drunk, drinking, doing drugs. But still He kept me alive. I have a friend that died in a car accident. I see people die from the things I did and I'm like, I didn't. I ain't die."

It's no secret that in the South even the most hardened of the hard are likely to have faith, though that might sometimes seem a contradiction to their surface behavior. But if that faith is not part of an organized setting, it's often looked down upon as less spiritually valid, which discounts a lot of people.

"God is not the church," says Chyna, taking care to make the distinction. "I could be sitting on a corner every day, just chillin'. But you don't know. I probably have a different relationship with God than somebody who preaches in the church. So the world is twisted. Once you see God and you start learning and knowing, then you gon' know and you gon' see. You gon' see the line. You gon' see the distinction. You gon' see the spirit. You gon' know you don't even have to play by the world's rules because the world may say no, but if God say yes, then it's yes.

"People in the church do some things that people in the street do," she continues.

"You know, they got more people in the 'hood serious about God than in a church. And I'm talking about God himself. But they got a lot of false prophets and false this and false that, believe me. Yes they do. That's why you have to have a relationship with God yourself."

Chyna now struggles to embrace a better path in life. Part of this includes finding ways to musically communicate her life experiences in a more positive manner that is true to her relationship with God. She's got a high-profile record label deal – her debut album is scheduled to be released jointly by Lil Jon's BME label and his partnership with independent powerhouse TVT Records – but she hasn't written much of it yet. She hasn't quite mastered how to portray this relatively new role accurately, and she doesn't want to rhyme about things that don't represent who she is now. So for now, she's taking her time to get it right.

> **She doesn't want to rhyme about things that don't represent who she is now**

"A lot of rappers I talk to, they are spiritual, but you would never know it," she points out. "A lot of people want to [put it in their work]. But I'm not gonna be that person that *want to*, I'm gonna *do it*, you know? I don't wanna be, 'Oh yeah, I wanna do it. Yeah, I love God. Thank you, Jesus' – but I'm on the song talkin' bout, 'I'mma bust your head and I'mma kill you, nigga.'

"I'm not judging nobody, because, look, I've been struggling hard to clean my raps up. It's just terrible," she laughs. "Every time I say I'm going in the studio and I'mma do something positive, do something good, I come out with the devil. So it's like, 'Okay Jesus!' But I know God is in my life and I know he speaks to me and I know he's bringing me to another level 'cos I can feel it, and I'm just like really that's my source. I depend on him and I know he's in control of everything. If it's my destiny to rap then I'mma gon' rap, no matter what."

Surely many artists share Chyna's challenge of making relevant music that doesn't contradict her present lifestyle yet still grabs the attention of those who need to hear her message most. But few have dared to speak up in a significant way without leaving the secular world entirely. In a landscape where the club-oriented songs are still the most popular, it's no easy feat to be righteous and totally free of vice. Importantly, Chyna realizes that she will do others no good until she's straight within herself.

"It's all about renewing my mind first," she notes. "It has to start with me. How can I help somebody if I'm not even different? So that's been my biggest focus, because the world is much more than women bending over and popping [champagne] bottles, you feel what I'm saying? You know, like, come on! People dying. There are kids out there that don't have parents. They killing each other. I know I don't want to be too serious but, hey – you've gotta realize it. Somebody gotta be serious."

It hasn't proven to be an easy transition for Chyna; in fact, she had even thought about throwing in the towel, but feels she was convinced to stay on track.

"I can't be nothing but real," she asserts. "I can't do nothing but what's in my heart. That's it. And really, I told God that I was not gonna rap. I really told him I quit. I said if I can't get my shit together and write I quit. I don't wanna do it no more. I quit. But He told me, 'No, you need to be heard. You need to be heard.'"

Chyna Whyte is, hands down, one of the most talented women in the rap game. She's a secure female who doesn't rely on selling sex to be heard.

"It's too many females out there that come out and they doing the same thing even if they intentions was, 'I'mma do this, I'mma do that.' But they wind up bent over or crouched or something. You know? It's like, come on. But I can understand what they're going through because it's a lot of influence they want you to do. And it's like, 'No, I'm not gonna be no eye candy, I'm sorry. No.'"

Not to say that she's not sexy, because she certainly is. But she stays relatively natural with it. She's got a clever tongue, too – what other lady would have thought to rhyme "ass clap" with ASCAP (the American Society of Composers, Artists and Publishers, from which she receives proper publishing checks regularly)? By escaping the common trap for women in hip-hop, where the male-dominated forces dictate micro skirts and perilous heels, Chyna has set a strong example for girls. These days, it's a responsibility she takes seriously, even taking the time to talk to such fans online.

"They look up to me, you know? I feel like I was on a road to destruction that I didn't even know. And I feel like God pulled me out of that and showed me where I was going and he saved me and he kept me here because I feel like I'm not better than nobody else. I've had a lot of friends die, get killed, get killed in accidents, die from sickness and I'm like, 'Why? Why not me? I'm no better than them.' But I feel like if God saved me and he showed me, then I need to show them. So that's been a big battle with me. I need to find somebody who's on the same page as I am because I'm the type of person that goes against the grain."

roughneck redeemer

"I used to thug a lot harder than these boys can rap about," says the luminescent Cee-Lo Green (Thomas Callaway). "And that's how I know that I was spared."

Cee-Lo, who came to fame as part of the Goodie Mob, can remember a time when he was the exact opposite of the man he is now. Before he assumed what *Village Voice* writer Greg Tate calls Cee-Lo's "feverishly roughneck redeemer persona," he was far more roughneck than redeemer.

"I hate for my music to come across one-sided, for people to think I just appeared out of thin air," he vents. "Here's an individual with so many positive things to say. They have to understand that my positivity comes from a lot of pain. I've endured a lot of pain." He deals with the internal struggle most prominently on the song 'Medieval Times (Great Pretender)' from his debut solo album, 2002's *Cee-Lo Green and His Perfect Imperfections.*

"At one point in time, I had nothing positive to say," he explains. "And, you know, I'm self-educated. I dropped out of school in the ninth grade and so typically I would either be dead or in jail. I was well on my way – that I can promise you. But since I have been spared, I want the thugs now to be able to see themselves in me and therefore they can see what a change you can make and what is possible. You got to depict it all."

He croons a line from Usher's R&B hit 'Confessions Pt. 2' for emphasis: "If I'm gonna tell it, then I gotta tell it all!"

Both Cee-Lo's mother and father were Christian ministers. His father died when he was young, and he credits the subsequent loss of his mother as his personal turning point in abandoning the thug life for something more spiritual.

"I think my mother and father are both watching me and I am full of their spirit and intention," he says. "My mother told me that my father once said that I would have something very special to do with my life. And so it's a fulfillment of prophecy, each day that goes by. I'm proud of that and I believe in God even more so because of what I had grown up hearing within life. And not even from them but from different people."

It's been almost a decade since the Goodie Mob released their first album, *Soul Food,* in 1995, establishing the group as a refreshing force to be reckoned with, and yet Cee-Lo is still not quite 30 years old. But he speaks with the clarity of someone twice his age, particularly when it comes to the ultimate source of his musical talent.

"My music is – its essence is one of the purest and most prolific manifestations of a God, of a higher power," he shares. "Divine intervention."

One need only listen to a note or two of Cee-Lo's extraordinary voice to understand that he does indeed have a heavenly gift. He's as multi-dimensional in the type of songs that he might tackle. Nowhere is this more evident than on his sophomore album *Cee-Lo Green is the Soul Machine*, as he runs the gamut from sharply lyrical hip-hop battle action ('Glockapella,' 'Childz Play') and sinister country blues ('Evening News') to soulful house music ('Livin' Again'). Perhaps the only Southern artist out there as experimental and ambitious in range is his Dungeon Family brother, OutKast's Andre 3000. Indeed they are two of the most important artists when it comes to reaching out of the region and right into the international musical community.

"I'm raised by a lot of different music," says Cee-Lo. "I'm *biased* about music! For some reason I gravitated towards what was quality in music [as a child]. Like, I know all about The Eurythmics, I know all about Madness, Dexy's Midnight Runners. You know – I grew up in the '80s. But it was good and I could feel it. Talking Heads' 'Burning

Down the House,' that was a hit. Who missed that song? Who doesn't know 'Everybody Wants to Rule the World?' At that time, the lines in music were blurred. I really, really soaked all that music up. I have a worldly outlook as far as music is concerned. I know there's a big ol' world out there."

Cee-Lo may make songs that span a spectrum of tone and mood, but for him it's all united by one single strand.

"Amidst all of that diversity and range, the common thread is, to me, the gospel. That's one thing you won't miss. Even if I'm not telling you. Even if it's not about anything remotely spiritual or religious, you will hear gospel in my voice. You will hear faith and conviction and hope and joy and pride and pain and love and happiness and all of that stuff."

It's one thing to realize that you have a God-given talent, quite another to know that this talent has a higher purpose than merely entertaining. There have been many artists who describe themselves as being a vehicle for God, but Cee-Lo's got a different twist on it.

"It just feels like the grace of God, because it's allowed me to be so much more at peace and has caused my life to be purposed and intentful. And so I don't feel like it's anything coincidental or random. I feel like I was thought about and called, so to speak. So more or less my music is the dance of deserving. That's what I call it. Trying to earn and deserve what God has given me, 'cos I truly don't know what I've done to have it.

"And so it's gospel for me because it's praise and I praise God for sparing me and giving me a clue, giving me an idea. So it is praise in that sense. And it is a sacrifice of wanting to be pleasing in the sight of my Maker. If anything, my music is between me and God, you know, and I guess people get a chance to bear witness to that relationship. I know that sounds pretty big but it's very, very simple for me."

Other people not only get to bear witness, but get to be affected by it, whether it's just on the surface level of pleasing musical sounds down to something deeper and more educational if they heed the message.

"A lot of my music is empathy," he reasons. "It's out of empathy for our conditioning and it causes me to want to create an alternative and an option that assures all that listen and hear that there is another way for me to go about it. I want to spread optimism and faith and hope with the medium of music. And so that's what the political stance and savvy comes from as well. I do believe there is an industrial genocide. I say this all the time but it never stops making sense that a capitalist society has to have somebody to capitalize on. So our ignorance is perpetuated.

"I'm willing to fight and sing and dance and die in the name of our change and our uplifting and empowerment. And the reason I can go as far as to say I'm a revolutionary and that being my cause is because I know that I am a threat to the establishment …"

Cee-Lo realizes that what he is doing is entertainment and that things are not always

so solemn. But that doesn't mean he will compromise himself in order to be more entertaining.

"That's what drives me no matter what my music is about. And it's also relevant to being from the South. It's that Southern intuition and kind of feel and soul and genuineness and sincerity. It's what you hear in the conviction. I mean, like, in the truth and the honesty and the humanity and the humility. All of these different things could be typecast as Southern qualities, know what I mean? That's my music in a nutshell."

By breaking down barriers of what would be accepted in mainstream hip-hop, Goodie Mob were meant to herald an era of artists who would continue with ever more frank discussion on the oppressed condition of the black Southern underclass. This era seems to be still somewhat in incubation, though it has grown significantly in the past 10 years in the lab.

A significant part of this period of new growth has to be the proliferation of crunk music and the associated lifestyle. Its underlying message may be implicit to someone like Cee-Lo, who sees the lineage to his own work as well as the future potential.

"The music that the young soldiers are doing, more commonly known as crunk music, with Lil Jon and the stuff that's going on, that is revolution in itself," he declares. "It's almost like I'm a soldier and an officer at a higher ranking. When you see crunk, when you see the young soldiers gettin' buck and gettin' crunk, that's everything that I *can't* say. That's why crunk music isn't about lyrics, it's about *feeling*.

"I was infantry at one time. I've survived a number of wars and battles. And here I am, delegating strategy for my soldiers to go to war with. And of course there are casualties in the process, but I don't send them off to die."

It's easy to be the devil's advocate and miss the merits of crunk as a long-term revolutionary strategy – certainly as long as it seems like many people are in it to get fucked up and/or bust some heads in a club. Don't tell that to Cee-Lo, however, for he senses success on the way.

"They hear me, know what I mean? But they are the action and the physicality of something that is outspoken or forseen. I believe that myself, Goodie Mob and the Dungeon Family, I think that we are the unspoken cause and fuel to that fire that is crunk music. Like it's that uprising and they have soldiers in the trenches and in the field.

"But just being young, you may not understand what that energy means. It's deeper than just the entertainment value, but it is entertaining to see. But I want to see cause and give them a higher purpose for their energy and direct it in a much more constructive way. To channel that energy is power, for it to be unbridled is chaos. I don't endorse the chaos.

"So what I do on another end of it, I'm there trying to help make sense of how you feel and why you feeling it. Crunk music is a sign of the times. They're gonna tear down these walls that bind us. I'll be there saying, 'Once the walls get torn down, then what?'"

For the most part, crunk seems to still want to linger in unbridled territory, so it's hard to assess how successful Cee-Lo has been so far in reaching the younger set. He is confident in the results.

"I'm watching them, I'm getting to them," he insists. "They know I exist for a fact, but it's their time and their energy and their youth: They have to get it out in that way. They have yet to go through the storm like I have in order to be able to reenter with great wisdom back in their direction. When you're young you just know how to go at it with your body, know what I mean?"

I ask Cee-Lo if he sees future leadership potential in any of the young stars of crunk. Fortunately he singles out one of the fastest rising talents.

"I had a talk with Lil Scrappy," he recalls. "Lil Scrappy is a young man that I got a chance to meet and spend some time with and he got his head on straight. I even told him and his crew, 'God helps thugs,' you know, 'G's up.' I was just talking to them and they were telling me that they were influenced by me and impressed and inspired by me. And I'm like, for real? You might not be able to notice because the music is not similar to what Goodie Mob did, [but] it's not supposed to be.

"Crunk is fun, it's a release. They don't necessarily see it the way I'm telling you it is. But once it's read [in this book], somebody who feels crunk is probably gonna read this segment and it's going to make more sense to them how they feel. When it could have just been innocently just the energy of the drum. It's tribal. You see these boys get crunk and it almost looks like Soweto. That's what it looks like. So they're not playin'. It's not necessarily for a cause *per se*, but I'll help them to give them the cause in order to be energized by and for it. That's what I wish to be."

> **'it's tribal – you see these boys get crunk and it almost looks like soweto'**

Cee-Lo Green is a modern missionary. Whether his words and music inspire listeners to strengthen their personal spiritual relationships, provide relief and relaxation from everyday stress or simply lead them to the dancefloor, it's all a positive impact.

"It's also therapeutic for me as well," he points out. "When I feel like I'm moved and attempt to say something positive, I can look back on my music and feel like I was being used and I feel pleased and purposed. I don't know quite what I've done to deserve it, so I try and live my life to continue honoring and deserving what it is that has been bestowed upon me: A grand blessing of music.

"It's the rough side of the mountain but I don't think God chooses weak individuals to do his work. So I am a soldier for the salvation army, no pun intended."

Cee-Lo recognizes that God gave him a talent to use early on in his career, but to this day he sometimes still questions the reason: "I'm like, why me?" But then, why *not* him?

"It makes me want to witness even more," he says. "Because who better to witness that there is a God than someone as imperfect as myself?"

the divine side

Cee-Lo and Chyna Whyte are staying on the secular side of the music business, while collectives such as Holy Hip Hop in Cee-Lo's hometown of Atlanta adopt the musical feel of crunk to deliver their spiritual principles. Holy Hip Hop, which has its own radio station (Atlanta's WHLE 106.3 FM, which broadcasts online via *www.live365com*), even features an artist called Sea-Lo! (While Cee-Lo hadn't heard of his veritable twin, he didn't seem to mind, perhaps given the positive subject matter.)

Down in Memphis, there's a particularly interesting artist exploring the divine side of hip-hop. "Over the last few years, a number of former secular artists have turned to the Gospel to express their musical talents. Perhaps few in that category have been as committed and have made such an impact as the likes of Mr. Del," writes the Web site *Gospelflava.com*.

Mr. Del – also known as Pastor Del to his congregation at his "hip-hop church," City of Refuge – came from a most unexpected place. Formerly part of the Three 6 Mafia crew (which has a name that technically is a bit at odds with "the good force"), Mr. Del was saved in 2000 and formed City of Refuge in the spring of 2001.

Music remains a backbone for Mr. Del and his message. He has established a record label called Holy South, which he likens to a kind of "Christian Warner Brothers." Several of his songs sound nearly identical to secular crunk records that might be heard at a club or on the radio, with one small exception. For example, while many artists shout out the word "bounce" as a means of hyping up the listener, Mr. Del has a song called 'Holy Bounce,' where the title becomes the new chant. Tunes are free of curse words and sexual content, but reach similar levels of pure energy.

"The South has always been noted as the Dirty South," writes Mr. Del on the Holy South Web site, "but we are people that are chosen by God; He has washed us with his precious blood and now are declared clean. So we are not the Dirty South, we're the Holy South."

Mr. Del also points out that his ministry was founded on *The Bible*'s 1 Peter 2:9: "But you are not like that, for you are a chosen people. You are a kingdom of priests, God's holy nation, His very own possession. This is so you can show others the goodness of God, for He called you out of the darkness into His wonderful light."

While he preaches at the Memphis-based City of Refuge, Mr. Del also has a traveling program called Refuge, which goes to different cities. He describes it as the ministry's "non-traditional and non-religious" "evangelistic department." It consists of three components: "Nu Soul," college events and seminars that use neo-soul and hip-hop as vehicles; "Holy South," which focuses on high schools, targeting them with both religious and secular rap shows; and "Uncut," a Bible study conducted in the hip-hop vernacular. In June 2004, Mr. Del was awarded the Peace Achiever of the Month in Memphis by local radio station K97.

"This ministry is the most radical movement of God seen to man yet," he writes, "and will be the most effective concerning the lost youth of today's dying world."

Time will tell, but the thing is, it wouldn't be surprising if Mr. Del is right.

"God I know that we pimp/God I know that we wrong/God I know I should talk about more in all of my songs/I know these kids are listening/I know I'm here for a mission, but its so hard to get 'em when 22 rims are glistening ..."
DAVID BANNER, 'Cadillac on 22s'

"Jesus died that we may live and live more abundantly," says Chyna Whyte. "It's so much more. I thought, 'Yeah, I got saved and it's just I'm saved, yeah, whatever.' But it's so much more than just that. It's just so much more and I just pray that I finish this album and it be everything that I prayed that it be and it will just help somebody. Whether it sell or not, whatever, you know, I'm just all about doing what God want me to do. I'm all about helping people get through they problems, they struggles, they depression. Because I've been through it and it's a fight. And when you don't know how to fight, it's horrible.

"Sometimes I go on a fast for like three days, no food, for other people. For God to help them and touch them. A lotta people ain't gon' give up they food for that. You know what I'm saying? It costs you. It may cost me everything. It might cost me my whole career, everything I've worked for. I've been rapping 11 years now. It might cost me everything, to lose all of that, to find God. And I'm to the point where if it costs me that, then I don't care. Then He can have it. And that's the point I'm at."

Her struggle is honest, hard work, and her perseverance should bear her through the bumpiest parts. From the sound of it, it already has.

Hard work is not a foreign concept to Southerners, especially those trying to survive and succeed within the sharpened steel jaws of the music industry. And since the leaders of Southern hip-hop have not been known to take the easiest path thus far, it may be up to them to definitively convey those internal debates and conflicts in a manner that helps others. Cee-Lo has some advice for those who confront similar issues and are attempting to steer in a positive direction, like Chyna Whyte. It is more forgiving advice than what might be found in most organized situations.

"You have to be human first and foremost," he offers. "And I think explaining and

Jacki-O: Bringing the Dirty South message into the mainstream.

expanding upon all that you are is a much more thorough lesson to be learned. You really get a chance to convey how powerful God is when it is evident how imperfect you are. And then, that way, you don't necessarily come across too good to be true. How you get your point across or what your intent is and where you're striving to go or what you're aspiring to be, just be consistent with it. And most likely you'll die trying, you know?"

Chyna says that, in the long run, she might prefer to stay behind the scenes as a writer. (A sharp businesswoman, she realizes that's also one of the most lucrative places to be.) Musically, she ultimately strives to craft the sort of fine gospel songs that someone such as Yolanda Adams might sing. She and her husband also have future plans for releasing and promoting other artists through their own company. In the meantime, she takes her responsibility as an artist seriously and is trying her hardest to become the most positive vehicle that she can.

Chyna Whyte may have thrown down that ax down a long time ago, but she's still ready to fight the good fight. "Somebody gotta step up," she says. "And whether they listen or not? Well, I just did my job."

ON THE VERGE

FEATURING I-20, Young Buck, Stat Quo and Jacki-O

Their moms named them Bobby, David, Stanley and Angela, but these four MCs have introduced themselves to the world as I-20, Young Buck, Stat Quo and Jacki-O. Coming from Georgia, Tennessee, and Florida, they have many perspectives to bring to the overall picture of the Dirty South. And people are listening. They're all real, hard working, intelligent Southern people with gifts to express and wisdom to impart. As they translate earned street cred to the mainstream, they move forward without compromising their essence.

Bobby Sandimanie originally called himself Infamous 2.0. A few years ago, he changed his alias to I-20, which is also the nickname for Interstate 20. This highway, running from South Carolina to Texas, is sometimes called "the Deep South's east-west main street." The newer moniker feels deeply connected to Sandimanie's intention to represent a different facet of what people understand to be Southern hip-hop, one that runs through its very core.

As part of the Disturbing Tha Peace crew, helmed by Ludacris, 20 has been there throughout the stages of his friend's rise to fame on a national and global scale. You can find him in just about every Ludacris video as support, whether rolling alongside him in 'Southern Hospitality' or chasing ladies in 'Area Codes.'

Musically, 20 debuted as a guest on Ludacris's road rage anthem 'Move (Bitch)' along with New Orleans' Mystikal, appeared on the Disturbing Tha Peace family album (2002's *Golden Grain*) and is a constant touring fixture with Ludacris.

He also popped up on a hit R&B song in the summer of 2004, Houston's 'I Like That,' along with Nate Dogg and Chingy. The song was featured in a McDonalds ad campaign and received heavy radio and video rotation.

Being the third person on two huge songs is great exposure, but it also brings a good taste of what it is to be near the spotlight yet not quite in it. 20 has often said that he encompasses the 'disturbed' component of Disturbing Tha Peace. Indeed, he forgoes Ludacris's ribald humor for a more serious delivery, rapping in a darker way on typical inner city tribulations. His name has gotten out there a bit and he's had a taste of fame because of these things, but 20 doesn't feel – or act – like a superstar, preferring a humble outlook.

"I think I got a decent fan base," he surmises. "When you're on the road with 'Cris, though, they're just there to see 'Cris. If you snatch one or two fans there in that time period, cool. But ultimately they're there to see 'Cris … I think that I've definitely started the initiation of starting my fan base. Am I at a point where I've got a fan base? No. But I'm building it. Because again, like I said, people who go for the main attraction, they're there for the main attraction. You go to see the Lakers play two years ago, you were there to see Shaq and Kobe. You didn't give a fuck if Derek Fisher dropped 30 points."

Surely, 20 is downplaying his position in the rap world just a little bit?

"I'm downplaying it, but I'm just saying that that's the reality. You better think about it like that, because it keeps you grounded. And that's one of those kinds of things where you're in just a love/hate relationship [between] an artist and the audience because you *feel* the audience. That's the part that you love. You feel the audience because that makes sense, but you hate it because sometimes it gets so intertwined in that, that they're saying 'fuck you' before you even get a chance.

"Especially when you're somebody like me that's associated with another rapper," he says, becoming more candid. "I can't fucking win. No matter what I do, I can't fucking win. I don't care what anybody says, I lost by being with 'Cris.

"Because 'Cris is so successful that I can't win. Because whatever I come out with, when I come out with it, ain't but one

> **he's seen success happen with ludicris, so you would think he'd know what to expect**

or two things gon' happen. Either they're gonna be pissed because they're gonna say in one instance, 'Ah, he just lacks the so on and so forth that we love from 'Cris,' and, 'Ah, it's not quite the same.' But then on the flipside, if I do anything [like his], they say, 'Ah, he just sounds like a generic Ludacris.' I can't win."

A generic Ludacris is very far away from what I-20 is as an MC, as evidenced on his debut album *Self-Explanatory*. His voice – deep and full-bodied, well described by several writers as "muscular" – is distinctive. It's hard to accuse him of trying to sound like anyone else, which will prove to be an asset in his career.

And unlike the artist known as 'Chris Lova Lova' in his radio days, I-20 makes sex only a small focus of his album, with the downright sweet 'Hey Shawty,' a flirtatious shout to ladies, featuring Houston's Devin The Dude, and 'Slow Fucking' with DTP's Shawnna. Songs like 'May Sound Crazy' and 'Kisha' are cautionary tales for the hood. Meanwhile, 'Fightin in the Club' (featuring DTP's Lil Fate and Tity Boi and Chingy), 'Hennessy and Hydro' (with the legendary Three 6 Mafia) and first single 'Break Bread' (featuring Ludacris and Bone Crusher) all speak about the more blunted and rowdy sides of social life. Those are more in the vein of 'Move (Bitch).'

"It's something I've always wanted to do, so I'm gon' be nervous about how the public responds," he admits. "Because you wanna believe that what you're doing is not in vain. You wanna believe that every time you ever told yourself, 'I can do this. I can be successful with this,' that the rest of the world was looking at it the same way. That they believed you could be successful as well. [Yet] you don't wanna sit down and believe all of this to a point where ultimately you're disappointed because nobody is gonna, you know, come see your music. It can hurt. It will hurt. Anybody who says it doesn't is lying."

It's interesting for him to say that he's nervous when he's seen all of the success happen with Ludacris and been right there by his side. You'd think he would know what to expect.

"When I say 'nervous,'" he clarifies, "I mean the kind of nervous like you are anxious, like you got a big trip coming up on Friday and you been waiting and saving up a year for it. It's more of an anxious than particularly nervous because it's like, 'Yo – I've dreamed this in my head a thousand times. I hope it is even 40 per cent like my dream.'"

For all of the messages contained within *Self-Explanatory*, 20 had something even more serious originally penned for the album, a song called 'I Pray For America.'

"It's a song that I wrote when I was in the studio recording something else and I was watching CNN," he recalls. "I love to watch CNN. And it was one of those debates – those debates are funny cause it's a bunch of muhfuckers that can't do shit about what's happening, so they just sit around and talk about it. I love that.

"And they were talking about Bush. This was right when we were about to go to war. And I got a beat playin' and I didn't know what I wanted to do with it, and I wrote it and like, I know niggas like me, I know they like their entertainment and their education separated. That's the reality. But every now and then if you can make a good album and there's a record like that on there and you get that muhfucker to listen, then they'll say, 'You know, this is some cool shit.'"

'I Pray For America' made folks at his label Capitol Records (home to top bands like The Beatles, Radiohead and The Beastie Boys) nervous, so it didn't make it on to *Self-Explanatory* in the end.

"It'll be on my second album … What I'm saying in honesty is, like, I pray for us to realize what we're doing wrong and change it. I hate it when I'm watching CNN and someone says something like that and someone goes, 'Oh you're anti-patriotic.' And I don't think it's anti-patriotic, I love this country as much as you do but I think we're fucking up. There's nothing wrong with saying we're fucking up. We're fucking up! And it's stupid to [act] like we never fuck up."

Knowing how closely the government appears to be watching rappers, he's quick to drop a disclaimer. (Just in case anyone is listening.)

"I'm not against our president," he says. "I'm not against our country. But, you know, here's a woman, she has an 18-year-old son or daughter and they about to die. Be a man and be honest about what they're over there dying for. If you feel that strongly about it. If you think it's that necessary, then say what the fuck it is, but don't feed me the bullshit about, 'America's fighting for our freedom.' Who's threatening our freedom?

"A lot of the people from my label were real sensitive about it at first when they heard the subject because I have shit in there like, 'We got satellites and OnStar for tracking a van/But you mean you can't find a single man in the land of Afghanistan?/We got sex education but they ban prayer in schools/Wake up and get aware, this shit is going too deep/You can't create a single job but you can sit and clone sheep?'

"All I'm trying to say is, it's not that I'm taking shots, I'm just trying to show you that our focus is off. We spent billions for NASA. I don't give a fuck what's out there before [we learn] what's going on right here! Your point of interest is immediately off already. So the whole record is just about that. It's just about a lot of the ironic shit. And I posted more of the ironic shit than I did the cynical shit."

'I Pray For America' typifies the level of discourse that 20 is capable of bringing out, yet he understands that he needs to start back a few steps to grab the attention of the people.

"I don't consider it a struggle," he reasons. "I consider it a part of life. Art imitates life. That's life, man. That's life.

"When you're talkin' to a girl and you get her number, you don't give her the whole shit when you first give her your number. She don't give *you* the whole shit. You kinda feel out how y'all gonna be. What audience is this? What type of girl is this?

"Because we all are like that. Any person with even 30 per cent of a brain that's a thinking, acting person can adjust to whatever their environment is, what the crowd is, what the person is. You tryin' to feel out what it is. [Because of 'Move (Bitch)'] people wanna feel like the music I'm doing is aggressive and energy-driven. And that represents a part of me, so I don't feel like I'm sacrificing anything when the first album is a majority of that. I don't consider it dumbing down my material as much as that this is a business and you gotta kinda give an audience what they're expecting from you. Kinda working their way into being comfortable with you."

His immediate environment has provided a strong example of how that can work,

JAZZY T's
CLUB HOURS
MON 12PM—CLOSE
TUES. 12PM—CLOSE
WED. 12PM—CLOSE
THURS. 12PM—CLOSE
FRI 12PM—CLOSE
SAT 3PM—CLOSE
SUN 3PM—CLOSE

CLUB POLICIES

DECATUR →

I-20: Raw, bold, and experimental.

showing that artists can be raw and bold and experimental and still take people with them.

"I'm from Atlanta, so I *love* OutKast. And so I totally believe that the music that OutKast is doing right now is what they've always wanted to do. But being from where we're from, they knew better than to just jump out. I believe that Andre and Big Boi was so talented, they was like, 'Here's the shit y'all wanna hear. We can do that in our sleep and make a classic album.' And they *did*.

"And what they really started to have a passion for is when they started to expand and do more and more and it got to the point where they did so well with the other material that you had to respect what they were doing. You had to.

"You gotta get people in there, get 'em in for the ride, give 'em what they want to the point they expect it and say, 'Yo, I'll fuck with you.' That's the hardest thing to do, is to get the rap audience to say, 'I'll fuck with you.' And what I mean by, 'I'll fuck with you' is that I'll fuck with you to the point that if you do something new, I'll give it a chance, you know what I'm saying?"

With world affairs remaining as they are, it's unfortunate that 20 has to reserve a song like "I Pray For America" for a future album in order to give people time to catch up to the point where they can take it as it is intended.

"It's ironic, but I'll do it. I'll do it for the sake of so that when that record comes out it doesn't get overshadowed. Because people ain't fuckin' with me anyway. So a record like that doesn't get heard because nobody fucks with I-20. I'll do that just so that people will fuck with I-20 enough so that when I start to say shit they say, 'You know what, I never thought about that shit like that.'"

Why does it take listeners so long to accept different things, especially from new artists?

"It's the same reason you go to a restaurant and it takes you 'bout the 10th time to try a new meal. That's human nature. You get comfortable. We get into a niche where consistency is a big deal. Especially in the music industry, and in major league sports. How we determine who's smart in school, you know. One person makes the A one day, makes four Fs after that, then we're not gonna be quick to say they're smart because we're like, 'You're inconsistent.' You know? Four As by this person and we're, 'Okay, he's smart.'"

He's up on what's happening currently in rap music by virtue of being out and about so much. But his musical tastes actually edge towards something a bit more headbanging.

"I don't even really listen to rap," he laughs. "Nah! That's the irony. And when I do, it's usually old shit. I just bought my first guitar. I'm a huge rock-n-roll fan. Whatever you wanna call it – rock-n-roll, heavy metal, whatever – I got way more discs of that than I do rap. I'm not sayin' I'm not a hip-hop junkie, 'cos I am. It's just that my hip-hop junkiness is all circa '95, between about '93 and '95.

"The constants in my CD changer is, like, Puddle of Mudd, Incubus, Pink Floyd, The Doors, Chili Peppers. I like rock-n-roll because they fortunately have a freedom we don't really have in rap. They get to explore and they get rewarded for that. You kind of get punished for that crap … I think you can bring more back for the music you're making by not only listening to hip-hop.

So 20's got his first guitar and is ready to raise a little hell?

"Got it! I'm loaded! I'm ready to go! I got my little dude that's gonna teach my lessons. Bring him on the road with me and I'm ready to go! Expect my fourth album and be ready to be like, 'What the *fuck* happened to him?!?'"

It's not so surprising to learn of 20's rock tendencies; there's something about the way he carries himself in performance that can easily reveal rock as part of his roots. But it does take shock certain people.

"I did an interview one time, a white girl was interviewing me that was impressed when I told her my playlist. She said, 'Well, how come you don't think that more black people [listen to] that?' I said, 'I really don't think that's fair for you to say that because rock-n-roll music is something that – it's something that's instrument filled and instruments cost money. I couldn't afford a guitar when I was growing up. Rap is free.

"So if you wanna know why most of these niggas do rap? It's 'cause rap is free! No way I could've been able to afford even a used guitar growing up … It's all relative. It's like, 'Why don't more black people play tennis?' These sports cost money. They cost the shit we just don't got. We stay in the neighborhood and shoot hoops. It's all area-specific. As these things become more simplistic and as the technology becomes more affordable and more available, I think you'll be surprised."

> '*i think you bring more to the music you're making by not only listening to hip-hop*'

20's timing is fortunate; his album is coming out at a time when Southern hip-hop is massively popular. He realizes that while it is an opportunity, it can also be somewhat of a double-edged sword to be lumped in with a lot of other artists.

"They need to classify it. They need to know if this is a drama, if this is horror, suspense, an action flick. They do the same thing with music. You know, I'm born and raised in Atlanta, so I remember when all of Atlanta was bass music. That was it. And if it wasn't that then nobody wanted to hear it. Then OutKast came in '93, '94. They changed a lot of things. But it was still good music, you know what I'm saying? The South had to embrace it.

"Well, I think the same thing is going on now. You know, hip-hop, we have a lot of trends *per se*. And you know the thing right now is crunk music. Crunk music is running the world right now. And I appreciate it! Being from the South, I love all the love we're getting, but I'm just saying I feel like I wanna do something a little bit different in there. And I think that the world has now kinda deemed that typical Southern music, that [crunk is] now the new bass music. They deemed that what you expect from the South. So I'm just saying I'm doing something a little bit different. I'm not against that. I just do something a little bit different.

"My job, now that we have broken through, I feel it's kind of my responsibility to let people know we've got more to offer than just what you had. What you had is fine, but there's other things down here. We're a lot more diverse than just that."

It's a far more common experience to talk to rappers who are in it strictly for the money and glory than to speak with someone like I-20, who seeks respect for his craft above everything. His main challenge is not to achieve platinum dreams, though he certainly wouldn't mind if it happens. Instead, he's concerned with furthering the musical dialogue.

"What's the point of getting a record deal if I'm just gonna do what everybody expects me to do? I'd rather just come out with one album and sell one unit and everybody leaves this muhfucker bein' like, 'What happened with I-20? Oh, he was nice. He can rhyme. His music was good,' and so forth and so on, rather than put out a record where I myself was embarrassed with the work I'd done.

"I'm not sayin' I don't wanna get paid," he points out. "I'm just one of those kinda muhfuckers that I'm saying, 'At what cost?'"

not a kid any more

The phone rings. Eyes pried open peep that it's before 8am on the West Coast. A publicist from G Unit, the crew and label spearheaded by the popular 50 Cent, is on the line from New York, asking if an interview with Young Buck (David Brown) can happen right now, instead of an hour

> 'what's the point of getting a record deal if i'm just gonna do what everybody expects?'

from now. A garbled plea to wait at least another half-hour is mumbled before the mental snooze button is hit for a few more minutes of rest.

It's absolutely and positively the last thing most people would expect to happen the morning after Young Buck had released his debut album *Straight Outta Ca$hville*, which would go on to peak at number two on the *Billboard* Top 100 Albums chart in its first month out. The first single 'Let Me In,' with its bold guitar slashes and even more brazen proclamation of arrival ("I know you're gonna let me in through this rhyme," he insists) has garnered countless spins on radio and video networks all summer alongside two hits from fellow G Unit brother Lloyd Banks. There's a visible ad campaign for the album in the major national hip-hop magazines, helping to generate an awareness of *Ca$hville's* title way before its arrival. Indeed it is one of the more anticipated hip-hop albums of the season.

My mental picture of Young Buck on his Tuesday night release date has him partying at a posh Manhattan nightclub. There are free-flowing waterfalls of Cristal and Hennessy, scantily clad women on his lap and gargantuan blunts blazing in the air. All night long, till way past the break of dawn.

Young Buck: "I wanted to represent my city."

Maybe that did happen, but he was definitely on the grind the very next morning, sitting in a Big Apple hotel room with a stack of media commitments to fulfil. Work to do, and no rest for a G Unit soldier. And thus the earlier than expected interview.

"It was a good day, man," he says of the previous day. "It was wild to hear my record selling out in so many different states on the first day. It was crazy. I knew it was a lotta bootlegging before my record was released but I felt like it was a quality record and I felt like the same people who bought the bootleg or got the bootleg were going back to get the album."

Buck is an appreciative fan of West Coast hip-hop, and no one seems to have had more impact on him than Tupac Shakur, whom he often cites as the man who made him really listen. *Vibe* even ran pictures of the two side-by-side to suggest their "separated at birth" looks. And for the title of his album, he pays tribute to another seminal force from the West Coast.

"I wanted my album to really just kinda like establish who I am, what I'm about, where I'm from," he explains. "I got the concept from N.W.A. [album] *Straight Outta Compton* – made it *Straight Outta Ca$hville*. I wanted to represent my city, establish myself with the industry and with the people and the world exactly what Young Buck is."

Young Buck grew up in Nashville, Tennessee. He calls his father a "crack fiend" and says on 'Let Me In' that he hasn't seen him in a decade. His father's absence put extra pressure on his mother, who had to raise not only him and his younger sister but the kids left in her care due to his aunt's addiction to crack as well.

"It was far from fuckin' *Silver Spoons* [a 1980s sitcom] or anything like that," he told *Allhiphop.com*, referring to his early days. *Ca$hville* captures Buck's upbringing in a town that, with his cocksure flow running through violent stories, sounds at least as cutthroat as Compton. Titles like 'Bonafide Hustler' and 'Prices on My Head' speak for themselves, reflecting a fast life and an uncertain future.

"The South ain't safe no mo', so get a gun," he raps on opener 'I'm a Soldier,' "and pray to God you make it to see 21."

"I ain't really lived a young childhood and experienced the whole young teenage thing that the average teenager do," he explains. "It was more serious for me from the beginning. You get the grown man from the beginning from Young Buck."

I ask if he wishes he had more time to be a kid, to be in touch with his child-like side.

"Nah man, I'm not a kid anymore," he insists forcefully. "I'm 23 years old so I feel like it was perfect because I'm dealing with grown men now and that's what I am. For me to have the experiences that I had at a young age, it kind of prepared me to have a little bit more of an advantage than the average youngster out here."

The instant man of the house, little David Brown took to the streets and selling drugs around the age of 12-13, about the same time he started rapping. It was from the older hustlers he got the nickname Young Buck. His ambition to take a serious shot at the music business was steadfast by the time he hit his mid-teens, when he got a chance to meet Bryan 'Baby' Williams of New Orleans label Cash Money Records.

"I met Cash Money back when I was 15, 16-years-old," he says. "They were the first cats that was established. From there I basically spent two, three years of my life back and forth between Nashville and New Orleans trying to make it happen." School was long gone.

Buck started running with Cash Money a little while before they really broke out into the national arena with their 'bling bling' aesthetic of platinum grills (both on their teeth and on their cars). He helped them behind the scenes to build the Cash Money image.

"The people I used to have around me from Nashville was showing love to the Cash Money clique on the strength of Buck trying to make it; making sure Buck gets to where he got to go," he says in his record company bio. "We provided the cars you see in that video [Juvenile's 'Ha']: The yellow Ferrari, the blue Jaguar. Things wasn't all the way right for Cash Money around that time and we respected that. We were blessed to have a little something so we added to their finesse in the beginning."

After a few years, though, Buck grew frustrated of watching while other artists received priority and he still had no plan to work on, let alone release, his album. The waiting game is an all-too common experience for artists on any number of record labels. "It didn't work," he remembers, "and I decided to go back to Nashville and start putting out independent records, building a buzz amongst my city for myself."

He not only went back to Nashville, he went back to the streets. He managed to put out his own independent album, *Thuggin' Til The End*, though it met with disappointing sales. The consequences of street life weren't far behind the hustle, as Buck learned when he found himself shot in the arm and thigh as a result of a break-in to his house. So by the time he heard from his friend Juvenile, with whom he had stayed in touch since departing the Cash Money fold, Buck was ready to focus harder on his creative side once again.

"Me and Juvenile established a relationship when I was there all the time and he decided to do his own thing, what he got popping now, UTP. I used to roll with him and I started doing that for like a year and a half, two years. It was getting rough on Juvenile financially so he told me, 'If you get an opportunity, take advantage of it.'"

Buck's big opportunity would result from a trip to New York with Juvenile, though it took a little while to materialize. While in town, they met with 50 Cent, who had just turned his buzz on underground New York mixtapes into a record deal with Shady/Aftermath, the labels run by Eminem and Dr. Dre, respectively, through the giant Interscope Records. At the time, 50 was working his multi-platinum debut album, *Get Rich or Die Tryin.*

Accompanied by G Unit's Lloyd Banks and Tony Yayo, 50 Cent came to visit Juvenile and Buck on Juvenile's tour bus, which doubled as a mobile studio. There Buck got a chance to freestyle and play them songs he had recorded. One song caught 50's attention so strongly that he asked him if he could join in and rework it for his album. It emerged on *Get Rich or Die Tryin* as 'Blood Hound.'

"The record kinda like took off from there for us and, you know, I looked at the situation with him always standing there in the middle with two of the best, Eminem and Dre. So for him to take my material, he ready to put it on his album, I knew it was a little bit more than just a feature song. I stayed in touch and he told me if his situation happened he was gonna come back and holler, and that's exactly what he did."

Signing with G Unit Records after the runaway success of 50 Cent was the real kick-start to Young Buck's career, yet there's someone else he's quick to credit.

"God is the maker of me and made my whole thing as far as being responsible for my career," he says. "I like to tell people to push. I push: I prayed until something happened. Everybody get they direction from praying. I wake up every day from prayers, yeah."

Then there are the Southern rappers that he's admired and befriended over the years, forming a supportive network that has helped bring him towards his goal.

"UGK – Bun B and Pimp C – they're probably the two that I really got a lot of game from. David Banner and Lil Flip, they always been around me, you know, before this year, kinda like giving me the game. And they know the business also, I've had a chance to learn from them, and learn from a lot of different dudes' mistakes out here."

A huge lesson he's learned is about unity and the importance of keeping G Unit tight and impervious to the obstacles that routinely befall rap crews. "We are family," he says of G Unit. "We just brothers from another mother, ma, that's it. We're one."

Buck has been to Europe twice, as well as Japan, on tours for 50 Cent and G Unit. The experience has opened his eyes wider to the world out there, even though he's had little time to spend in each place so far since they move by jet.

"It's been cool to watch music break the language barrier, you know? People can rap

> 'i look at it all as a blessing – it's fun for me to be able to see more of the world'

with you on stage but the minute the show's over they can't tell you what's up because they don't know how to speak English, so it's cool." A highlight of his recent visit to Europe was Iceland, catching the tiny country during the time of year when it offers 24-hour daylight.

"I'm pretty much just having fun with it. I'm enjoying it. I look at it all as a blessing. It's fun for me to be able to see the world, yeah, it makes me want to see more of the world."

Just before the interview, he completed the video for *Ca$hville's* second single, "Shorty Wanna Ride," which loosely mirrors Oliver Stone's murder'n'mayhem flick, *Natural Born Killers*. After coming up with the concept, he wants to do more for future videos.

"I wanna be involved in as much of my career as possible, so you can look forward to seeing my name right beside the director's on the videos pretty soon," he says. As for other business ideas, he's got some in mind, but he wants to first concentrate on the music.

"I'm going to work the record to the top of my potential, let the record go as far as it can go. And this record is a stepping stone to jump off into other different things that I'd like to do as far as making money with the [tire] rims and putting G Unit South Records together and everything, just making a lot more albums."

"As long as we're making good music, I think we'll be here. It's about making quality music," he concludes. "Whether you're from the East or West Coast, South, wherever."

At the time this book went to press, however, Young Buck's immediate future was uncertain. He was facing a charge of assault with a deadly weapon, following a incident at the *Vibe* magazine awards in Santa Monica, California, in November 2004. Buck is alleged to have stabbed a man who approached and punched his friend and producer Dr. Dre. If convicted, he was facing a prison sentence of up to eight years.

not your average rapper

Stat Quo (Stanley Benton) has that certain look in his eye. The one that suggests that he'll topple over anything that stands in his way.

I should know, because he damn near knocked me to the ground (accidentally, of course) while moving into the crowd during his live set at a showcase for Atlanta's annual Atlantis Music Conference. There aren't very many in the house, probably due to the club's lack of liquor license, but Stat honors his obligation with a set worthy of a much more packed room.

He charges into his street hit, 'Problems,' a staple on many mixtapes and a feature of the latest installment of his own *Underground Atlanta* mixtape series. His delivery is instantly arresting; it only takes about five seconds before catching on to the vibe that interested Eminem and Dr. Dre enough to sign Stat Quo jointly to their Shady and Aftermath labels (where 50 Cent is a label mate).

Sometimes his words seem to get angrily gnashed in pursuit of making a point you can feel. He aims for no less than lyrical domination; the passion and strength in his voice is always on the surface.

Stat's T-shirt reads, "I'm a fuckin' star." I'm not one to disagree.

A few days later, I'm ringing the bell at his house. Nitro, who served as Stat's hype man at the showcase but is an up and coming artist in his own right, answers the door. LT Moe, producer of 'Problems' and several other Stat cuts, runs through different sounds in his sampler downstairs in the studio. It's immediately clear that not only is it a family vibe here, but the household is a strong reminder that hip-hop isn't just something to do, it's something to live and breathe, 24/7.

With a Bachelor's degree in economics and international business from the University of Florida, the 26-year-old is clearly not your average rapper: He's a student of the game. Stat moved back to Atlanta just as the Def Jam South label was emerging with Ludacris. Inspired by how the local guy done good, Stat put together a demo and sent it to Scarface, head of Def Jam South.

Scarface didn't sign him, but he has remained a trusted figure in Stat's life. "He's a mentor," says Stat. "He's been where I'm trying to go. He's seen the ups and downs, the ins and outs of this shit right here."

What, I wonder, was the most valuable advice he's gotten from Scarface so far?

"He told me to get a girlfriend before I start," he laughs. (His girlfriend is upstairs, fending off strep throat.) "Not necessarily to get a girlfriend," he clarifies, "but to get those people that – to get your core people right now. Pick it wisely and get your team together. Because after a while you're not gonna know who's really down for you."

With a few notable additions, including his business partner and manager Zeek (with whom he's established Grown Man Music), Stat seems like he's got a good support system in place. And, in the case of Eminem and Dr. Dre, he's got two of the strongest co-signers in the business when it comes to establishing new stars.

Stat was able to draw significant attention to himself through a promotional tool commonly used by DJs, his *Underground Atlanta* mixtapes. In fact, it was through copies of *Underground Atlanta* being handed separately to Eminem manager Paul Rosenberg and Dr. Dre (through a former collaborator, Mel-Man, who met Stat via a mutual friend) that the two hip-hop moguls became interested in him.

The mixtapes proved to be a good business move for Stat, who used his own money to get the ball rolling.

"I just looked at it from the standpoint of any business you get into, there's two things you need to know. You're not gonna make money in the beginning of a business, and to create a demand for your product you have to create a supply. Understand what I'm saying? So I just saw that the only way for me to really get on and to make people notice me was to create a fan base. And the only way for me to do that was to put my music out on the street."

He reasoned that doing all of this legwork himself would be immeasurably more attractive to a label trying to sign him than if he were just one of many rappers out there. It was also a clever twist, in that mixtapes, again, are typically the DJ's domain.

"When you invest in yourself, a company, they see that and they respect that," he notes. "Because they feel like if you're willing to invest your own finances into yourself, you have a belief in it. And what people don't understand is that you've gotta be self-contained. People respect that in business. When they know that you would get out here and do everything you need to do, then they can just relax and be like, 'Well, we'll just add a little bit to it.'

"They're already moving in the direction they need to go. I attribute a lot of what I did on my own to my crew initially as the reason why I got a deal. Not to mention – I do my thing, but I definitely think they saw the work ethic in me and they said, 'Okay, this is a muhfucker we can fuck with.'

"The days of just doing a demo and waiting for somebody to sign you is over with," he continues. "Because me, as a business man, I don't wanna sign someone that just sent me a demo, because what are you doin'? You're not creating a fan base. Who's gonna buy your

Stat Quo: Not your average rapper.

record? I have to create the whole fan base for you? No way. Fuck that. Nobody's gonna buy your album if no one knows who you are. You can make a million songs in your house and let all your homeboys hear it. But if your enemies down the street don't know nothin' about it, or don't know anything about what you're doing, it doesn't matter to me.

"See, I make music for people that *don't* like me, you know what I'm saying? The people that already like me are gon' buy it anyway. I make music for the people that don't like me."

The first tape Stat ever bought was by Ice T; he counts the rapper, along with Scarface's Geto Boys and Dr. Dre's N.W.A., as chief influences. How amazing it must be to count two of your biggest heroes as mentor and collaborator.

"I definitely feel like I have a great responsibility because of who I am affiliated with," he reveals. "I'm dealing with the greatest producer in hip-hop history in my opinion. I'm dealing with one of the greatest MCs in hip-hop history [Eminem].

"To be in the room with them two, like, I just sit back like a little boy. What's so crazy is that they're so cool. They're so fucking cool, you wouldn't even think Em's sold over 30-something million records and you wouldn't think Dre's worked with Pac, Ice Cube and 50 Cent. Everybody's down to earth.

"And I see why they signed me from a personality standpoint, and from a music standpoint, because we all gel. We all have similar likes and dislikes when it comes to the music. We're similar people. You can't make music with people that aren't like you. The music won't come out authentic."

You also can't make music with people whom you can't stand to be around for as long as it takes to create a song. Especially if it takes a few days. With Dr. Dre's famous work ethic, there's probably a shower in his studio to facilitate living in there. "Yeah, there's a shower in there, so you have no reason to leave! And they bring the food and everything. You just sit in there working."

Of course there will be cynics who might say that Eminem and Dr. Dre signed Stat Quo simply to capitalize in the boom in national interest for the Dirty South. However, he can counter that accusation pretty quickly.

"They signed me because … of course they saw the earning potential in the situation. Of course. Let's not be stupid. But at the same time, they were looking at [signing me] anyway. They didn't know where I was from. Dre told me he thought I was from the West Coast. Because my sound is not in a box; I rap over every kind of beat, and I make my flow fit to the track. And then I make that track my track."

Eminem and Dr. Dre have a good track record for breaking artists, but they haven't shot out with 100 per cent accuracy all of the time. Though odds for success are good, nothing is a guarantee. It must be a tremendous form of pressure for someone in that position.

"It really don't get too much more pressure than when your life's on the line," Stat told *Hiphopgame.com.* "This right here, this is good pressure. This pressure don't kill you right here." Talk about having a proper perspective.

There's an annoyance that also comes with the territory, and that's handling people who want to create conflict, or 'beef.' And since Eminem and 50 Cent have gotten into high-profile beefs with other rappers, there will be people who will try to test someone like Stat simply just by association. He's prepared to handle it rationally and with a measure of grace.

"That just how it is," he concedes. "When you affiliate yourself with anyone, you take on their beef. I was down in Orlando with Em and Dre like a week ago, and Em was letting me hear his album.

"And he was playing this one particular record where he was talking about the different beefs, the different problems that people have with him … and how with 50 and the beef with Ja [Rule] all that shit fell on him and all that kinda stuff. It's like, a lot of times you don't even be involved in what's going on and people try to throw you in the mix.

> **'the days of just doing a demo and waiting for somebody to sign you is over with'**

"See, me? I don't have a problem with anyone. I don't have a beef with anyone. I don't want a beef with anybody because that's not my thing. I ain't into that. I'm here to make my music, make my money and make a way for my people to better themselves. All that talk about people dissin' this person and that person. You won't hear Stat Quo doin' a record about anyone. Leave people alone! I don't want none of that.

"Now sometimes, there's been cases where there's some personal shit between two individuals, and that's none of my business. I just know about me … I just want to make my music. I'm trying to better myself. This music has been an opportunity for me to get out of certain situations that I was in prior to it. And it's made a way to where I can come outside of my house and not see people across the street taking pictures. It's just a better move for your boy. It's a better look. Man, who wants to go to jail? Who wants to do that? It's a bad look!"

Ego is at the heart of the proliferation of beef in hip-hop in the present. Stat sees a lot of it as fairly unnecessary.

"The bigger your ego gets, and the more people love and embrace you, you have a harder time dealing with muhfuckers that's against you," he says. "You take it more personally because all you're hearing all day is praise. But when somebody doesn't praise you, you're so quick to get on the defensive. My thing is, muhfuckers don't have to like me. I don't care. It doesn't matter. But you will respect me. You will not disrespect me as a man. And I'm not gonna do a record about you, because that does nothing for me. In actuality, that helps you.

"I'm not gonna do a record about you," he says. "But what I *will* do is slap the shit out of you when I see you. But [as far as] doing a record? It's not gonna happen. Forget about it."

We change course a bit and start talking about the selling power of rap in the South, and how artists can move hundreds of thousands of units without ever having to leave the region. Stat's approach is different, as he's releasing to a national audience pretty much off the bat, but he acknowledges how there are some artists who choose to keep it local.

"It's like, if you grew up in a small town, and you never left your town, the world to you was that town, that's all you know. You never left. You never seen and went out to different places, you don't give a fuck about everywhere else. You don't care, you just care about your town, your people loving your shit …

"I just choose to make music for my town, your town, everybody else's town. I want my music to touch everybody, because I feel like I have a message for the world. My message is not for just where I'm from. And I want people to know where I'm from outside of certain areas. But there's nothing wrong with somebody making music just for the people around them. There's nothing wrong with that. Because if that's what makes them happy and that's what pays their bills, it's all good."

Before Stat drops his debut album *Statlanta* (featuring production by Eminem, Dr. Dre, Lil Jon and LT Moe) in the first quarter of 2005, he is guesting on songs on both Young Buck and Eminem's albums. Both of these feature spots give him a widespread introduction to many hip-hop listeners that he hasn't yet reached on his own.

While he's got a worldly outlook on life and his music, he's still representing the Dirty South and wants to shed light on more of the region's skill and talent with what he's doing.

"I feel that when people get exposed to Southern music, they just see it as one-sided," he told *Hiphopgame.com*. "They just think it's all about partying, they forget about some of the messages these artists put in their music. We party and have a good time in the South, we get crunk, but there's a lot of messages and storytelling. We're some real lyricists down here, and I want to expose that and make that more mainstream."

With so much light thrown on the South and so many artists getting record deals, there could be a danger of the mainstream burning out the South on a national level.

"No, I think the talent will stay around," he counters. "I think if you're talented you're not gonna have a problem," he reasons. "But I think if you're a bad rapper, you're just a here today, gone tomorrow type rapper, you're not gonna be around.

"It's not just about records anymore. People buy individuals and they like interesting people. And if people can't feel your personality and feel who you are through your music, and you're just saying, 'Hi, I'm Southern Man,' that shit ain't gon' run. You know what I'm saying? 'Who give a fuck, Southern Man! I don't wanna buy your album. [Get] the fuck outta here, dog.'

"It's just like anything," he observes, reaching for a historical analogy. "I think it was Queen Elizabeth, back in the day, she used to come out on the porch like once every three months and address the crowd. [One time] she came out, and this time she threw out tulips. So everybody in the crowd's like, 'Oh! Tulips is the shit!' So people just stopped growing all the other kinds of crops. They just started growing tulips and all these tulip stores popped up and everybody sold tulips 'cos that was the big thing. Then three months later, she came out with daisies. Now didn't nobody want tulips, so the whole city went into a depression trying to follow the fad.

"So, I say that to say, if you're just on a bandwagon, fucking with some bullshit, you're not gonna be successful – because this game is finicky. I feel like, me, I'm gonna be around for a long time."

a whole other entity

The sexy Jacki-O (Angela Kohn), fuel for so many men's fantasies, and I are in B.E.D. with a bunch of other girls and a couple of cats with a lot of gold teeth.

That's South Beach nightclub B.E.D., to be more precise. Jacki is shooting the video for 'Fine,' the first single off her debut album *Poe Little Rich Girl*, which finally saw release in October 2004 after almost a year of delays and shifts in her record label situation.

Mid-shoot, I've stumbled onto the set, a club dotted with beds that's actually one of Miami's popular party spots. Jacki has just finished her first dance sequence, and she's heading out of the club, cocktail in hand, to slip out of her barely-there shredded jeans into something more comfortable for the next shot.

I'm looking all disheveled, though still representing in my Compton Cheerleading T-shirt, no makeup, flip-flops and 5?2? glory. For some reason no one mistakes me for one of the video girls or asks me to jump in a shot with the tall, curvy, tanned and artificially endowed ladies hired to bump and grind behind the song's featured guests, Ying Yang Twins Kaine and D-Roc.

Rehearsal for their scene begins, and Kaine shouts, "Can we get some music? The girls need motivation!" As the Twins run through their lines several times, the video girls battle each other for prime camera space. In a way, they seem to mimic the hilarious posedowns normally associated with bodybuilding competitions. I'm on the opposite end of the room, but I'm pretty sure I see one girl yank another's weave to mark her perceived territory.

One statuesque girl removed from the first few takes for complaining about being too hot comes back in, only to topple backwards, stilettos over head, after smacking her ass to punctuate a line about smacking ass in the song. The room explodes in laughter.

Jacki-O's first video, for the regional hit 'Nookie' (known as 'P°°°y (Real Good)' in its explicit version) was banned from MTV and BET in 2003, though it's admittedly hard to see why the latter chooses not to air it when it is far tamer than many videos that appear on *UnCut*.

In fact, it seems like downright hypocrisy when compared to the motorbooty Olympics happening in videos from male rappers on the late night program. Men also routinely turn in songs much rawer than 'Nookie' to less attention and criticism than greeted Jacki's song about girl power.

"I wanted to put something dirty out there, as far as getting myself in the door," she

Jacki-O: "I wanted to do a nasty song and send a message."

explained to website *Gallery of Sound*. "But at the same time, I wanted to do something empowering for women. I wanted to do a nasty song and send a message. Some people have written it off as a gimmick or a novelty, but those same people are coming back to me now and going, 'Girl, I didn't know you had it in you; it's good!' I've been compared to other female artists that have had those types of songs, and that's cool 'cos those artists have pushed a lot of units, but Jacki-O is a whole other entity."

A little controversy, especially one as minor as this, never really hurts. Predictably, the video ban resulted in building up an extra air of mystique and anticipation for the release of *Poe Little Rich Girl*. Still, they weren't going to push it with the 'Fine' video, which politely stays within the normal bootylicious video standards.

Jacki stresses that there's no bad blood with Warner Brothers, the company which initially planned to distribute *Poe Little Rich Girl* (released on her Miami- based label Poe Boy) in early 2004. But she is happy that she and Poe Boy have gone to independent label TVT Records, where she could enjoy more than just a distribution deal. It would prove to be a place that would also give her an extra marketing and promotional push.

It also allowed her some extra time to tweak and strengthen her record, which includes production from in-demand producers Timbaland, Jazze Pha, Scott Storch and others and guests ranging from fellow Miami rapper Trick Daddy to legendary soul singer Betty Wright. Sure, she is sassy, nasty and steel tough at turns, but she's also incredibly funny and animated with a gift for entertaining. She's as versatile as her album's backing beats, which flit from electro-party grooves ('P°°y (Real Good)') to a slower string-led number ('Sleeping With The Enemy').

In all, her first few years in the business have afforded Jacki a crash-course in music industry politics, one that has improved her own approach to handling her affairs. That, plus her inherent hustler savvy, has taken her far.

"This game right here is so serious," she says. "I've met a lot of different people throughout my life and I've done a lot of different things to make money throughout my life but this game right here is so serious 'cos it's all legal. Once you sign something, by law you've given people rights to do whatever it is you sign. Ain't no contesting it, ain't no fighting it. So you have to know what it is you're signing. If you don't know, it needs to be explained to you.

"It's a serious game and there are so many sharks and egos and different personalities and people that actually just prey on you and get your money. And I'm talking about people in the industry and out of the industry. A lot of people come your way to see if they can just take something from you.

"You have to know what people are gonna do for you and pray to God they're gonna do what they say they're gonna do. You can rap till your tongue fall off, if you ain't got a successful team around you, if you don't have a team around you that's gonna make you a successful artist, you're rapping in vain. You have to be surrounded by a team, everybody around you has to fight for you."

Growing up in Miami's Liberty City, a neighborhood far removed in flavor and circumstance from the tonier South Beach, Jacki (who takes her alias from former first lady Jacqueline Kennedy-Onassis) has always had an appreciation for the local rap heroes. There have already been more than a few attempts in the media to inflame a rivalry between Jacki-O and Trina, Miami's most successful female rapper. If there is one, Jacki has taken care to be diplomatic about it in interviews, but you will hear subtle jabs here and there on *Poe Little Rich Girl.*

"I've always listened to Trick [Daddy] and Trina and JT Money and Luke Skyywalker," she offers. "I've always listened to them and feel like they've done a great job, but I have something to say as well and I want to be heard."

Before they hear her, people *see* Jacki-O. The petite, voluptuous MC has drawn comparisons to Lil Kim, though it has to be said that Kim shows more modesty overall in her style of dress. To call Jacki a sexpot somehow seems like a huge understatement. Jacki says that everyone, from interviewers to fans to DJs, ask her whether she likes being sexy.

"They think that I made myself wear the clothes or talk the talk or whatever but that's just actually me," she says. "I've always been – well actually, back in junior high school I was a little tomboy. I didn't even go to school. I'd sit in the hallways and just rap all day with my other friends, girls and other guys. We'd battle against each other, rappin'. We always wore sneakers and I started getting older and I started seeing

> **to call jacki-o a sexpot somehow seems like a huge understatement**

when the boys like it when you got on heels and boys like the little skirts. It was like, man, I gotta do what the boys like! You grow and you start feeling sexy about yourself and you wanna be sexy, you start loving yourself."

She acknowledges that the music industry is only too happy to pressure a female to sex up her presentation when it comes to developing an image. Women who resist this tide are few and far between.

"Right now you're gonna have to be a very, very powerful lady to actually pull that one off and say, 'Well, I'm not dressing sexy. I'm gonna dress in boy clothes and I'm gonna jump it off.' You gotta really hold it down to be able to do that. To me, I'm not doing it because it's a gimmick and I know that's what people like. I do it because I like to do it and this is me. But, you know, women are supposed to be sexy. Straight up, you're a girl: Like girlie things. And I'm not saying all women. I'm saying as an artist there's a thin line between, oh, I'm gonna be an artist and I ain't gonna dress sexy. You've gotta want every women to be you and every man to be with you and I know that and, like I said, it's gonna take a very powerful woman to try to say, 'I ain't dressing like that.'"

The Ying Yang Twins with the author.

She is forthcoming, however, with some notable examples of women who have defied the formula and pressures with a strong presence.

"They've accepted Da Brat, she doesn't wear short skirts, and they've accepted Missy [Elliott], and Missy doesn't wear short skirts. And these are two very beautiful women. They're powerful and they have a nice flow with it and I'm not saying it can't be done, I'm saying it's gonna take a very powerful woman and she has to be down in her own little category to do that.

"A man only looking at one thing. To me, a man ain't gonna look into your brain because your brain is not on display, your body is. And they wanna look at something nice. And a woman who's gonna represent for women, they ain't gonna want you representing when you looking all beat down and everything. So you gotta have your shit together. So that's why I'm saying all of that because I think the Missys and Da Brats, those girls, they hold their shit down.

"And I ain't saying be a sellout, but if you wanna be a successful artist you're gonna give people what they want and that's just point blank. I mean you can debate – 'I ain't doing this and I ain't doing that' – but you ain't gonna get no work. You know, if you wanna be so political about it you won't get no work.

"Bottom line is [if] you give the people what they want, there won't be no problems. I mean to be honest with you there's a love for music but I'd say there's a large percentage of artists that wouldn't be rapping unless there's a check involved in it, understand what I'm saying? I mean, if you're trying to eat and feed your family, give the people what they want. Give the people what they want. Be real about it though, never compromise being real, but give the people what they want. You'll eat."

She has recently tried her hand at acting, appearing in films like *Hustler's World* and *Tough Love*, and looks forward to future business opportunities in movies and beyond. But the music will stay her first priority.

"I guarantee you, if I was just a girl, I wouldn't get as much jobs if it weren't for the music. So the music first and that's how you get all the jobs. You gotta put the music time in there first and be a success and the other jobs and projects will come along, the roles and the endorsements. I've even been modeling Indigo Red, I'm the lead model for their clothing line. And I just got another call last week from some ex-Miami Dolphin players that want me to be a model for their clothing line, but it'll be a Jacki-O version of clothing that I'll assist in designing. None of that would have happened if it weren't the music first."

Someone that she considers a mentor in the business is Queen Latifah, whom she's never met. Latifah has not only had longevity in the music world, but is firmly established as a legitimate star of film and television as well.

"I don't make it a point of watching other people's careers, but as a female Queen Latifah's career kind of like stuck out for me. Just remembering her from back in the '80s with Monie Love and all these little girls and she's still out there doing her thing."

Jacki also enjoys a broader range of music than most might expect from her. In fact, she seems to name check almost everything but rap.

"I like alternative, I like rock, I like heavy metal – I like all kinds of music. I like Björk, I like Alanis Morrissette, Nine Inch Nails, Red Hot Chili Peppers, R&B, soul, Sade. I like all kinds of music, especially if it has a message in it and especially if it's narrative, like if it's telling a story."

It's time to catch a plane, and as I'm gathering my things Jacki is posing for promotional photos. She stretches out elegantly across one of B.E.D.'s beds, radiating an intense gaze from behind her shades. A stylist fluffs out her silk blouse, while a makeup artist powders her face. Ying Yang's Kaine howls appreciatively, and tells her to stick out her ass a little more.

Which may very well be the bottom line for a great deal of men who will take her in, a fact she will continue to work to her tremendous advantage. Pimp yourself, or get pimped. She's the mack. At the end of the day, Jacki-O is entering the fray with a clear vision about her career. It may be through false eyelashes and a couple layers of eye shadow and mascara, but her eyes are definitely focused on the prize.

"To me, success isn't money," she says. "It's doing something in your life and actually loving what you're doing and actually growing with it. To me, that's success. I just wanna be heard right now. I have a lot to say. And I want people to feel where I'm coming from.

"Right now I'm very confident in what I'm doing," she asserts. "I wouldn't want to be doing anything else in my life right now but what I'm doing right now. And I'm very, very confident and I know I have what it takes and I know I can get the job done. And I think as far as representing for the South – I mean, I ain't boasting, but I feel like I'm the best candidate right now. That's just it."

LIVE AID

FEATURING **Ludacris**

Mainstream hip-hop is known for its material trappings and glorification of the luxury culture. It's thanks to this lifestyle that those of us with substantially less paper know the model names of the latest six-figure automobiles as well as what to call the fine French champagne that, once upon a time, was merely a drink of the European aristocracy.

It explains how bargain shoppers can nonetheless be conversant with *haute couture* fashion houses. Sometimes it's even how we get wind of the latest electronic gadget – who else wants a Sidekick? – or, occasionally, which velvet-roped palace is the new 'it' club. Call it the University of Conspicuous Consumption.

Despite the money flying around, hip-hop is unfortunately less renowned for its charitable side or for helping in some way to renew the communities that inspire the art. This is not a subject typically tackled in videos, for instance. It's just not as sexy to show an artist at a soup kitchen, serving dinner to the disadvantaged, as it is to depict a nightclub filled with grinding girls.

Southern hip-hop likes to get its shine on, too; there's no sense in denying that. On the whole, though, more humble backgrounds overall do encourage a somewhat more restrained (and sometimes more conscious) form of boasting in Dirty South rap. They also explain why there are stars down South who may be on their way to leading the hip-hop nation someday when it comes to giving back.

When I caught up with Ludacris in Los Angeles in 2003, our interview for *Flaunt* magazine took place in a brand new Porsche Cayenne SUV. The plates had yet to arrive. As we chatted, it was hard to not be blinded both by his drive and ambition and by his platinum and diamonds.

"Look out for the medallion/My diamonds are reckless/Feels like a midget is hanging from my necklace!" he shouts on his hit 'Stand Up.'

The iced-out skull hanging from a thick platinum chain around his neck is the size of my fist, while his link bracelet, earrings and rings are all nothing to sneeze at. I calculate that the cost of these items might roughly equal that of my apartment (in one of the most expensive places to buy property in the country). Dazzling, to be sure, and a lot of sparkle for someone who has plenty of it naturally.

I also knew, however, that in addition to this tendency to be flashy, Ludacris has one of the kindest hearts in the business when it comes to his fans. This thoughtfulness is something he seems to extend throughout his travels as much as he can. Some of the further-flung places he's been have been documented by MTV specials.

On a one-off travel adventure edition of the MTV program *Cribs*, Ludacris headed to South Africa for a couple of days of vacation fun, but made a visit (and subsequent donation) to a youth community center in a particularly poor area. And in his episode of MTV's *Diary*, he explained how he took the bras and panties thrown onstage during one of his concerts in Jamaica and donated them to a local shelter for women. Who else would even think of that?

In 2004, a 17-year-old young lady from Springfield, Massachusetts, who is confined to a wheelchair with cerebral palsy wrote a letter to BET (Black Entertainment Television). She talked about how much she loved Ludacris and how she had no date for her senior prom. Guess who arrived in a white limo to take her to that prom?

The non-profit Ludacris Foundation, which started in December 2001, is the most beautiful manifestation of his care. Based in Atlanta, its efforts are centered there, although it has helped out in places like New York, Miami, Washington, D.C. and Chicago. "The Ludacris Foundation is an organization that's geared towards helping kids help themselves," explains Ludacris. "We take on a number of different projects – it's not like we're held to just one thing."

In Atlanta, the Foundation has hosted meals for hungry people at Thanksgiving and Christmas and has helped local programs such as Rah Rah's Village of Hope, Bankhead Courts Community Center and The Study Hall. It has also presented a pilot program at Atlanta's Southside Comprehensive High School, offering a course in Hip-Hop Culture 101, taught through music and dance.

"I also go to hospitals with rehabilitation centers for kids, so they can see me in person, and a lot of places like that," he says. "We did a homeless drive in Miami. I do inspirational speeches in schools and just try to tell them that education is important. We have a yearly event that goes on the weekend of July 4th in Atlanta and we give away food to different kids. And we just do a lot of different things as far as sponsoring boys and girls clubs, helping kids get uniforms for certain basketball teams. We try to do as much as we possibly can.

> **i calculate that the cost of this jewelry might roughly equal that of my apartment**

"[I'm] just getting out there and really touching people face to face. Because they see me on TV all the time and they see me out and about, but a lot of kids can't necessarily see me in person. So I think it's important to take time out of my schedule at least to go see some kids and give them autographs or just, you know, try to make their day. So that's important.

"It inspires me because I have a real soft spot for kids that are handicapped, in wheelchairs or crutches or kids that have to stay in a hospital and can't really get out. It just like touches my heart like really, really deep. It's just – man, it's just a real hard soft spot right there."

I tell him I think it's amazing, particularly because a little of his time means a life-long memory to someone else. (I should know, for interviewing someone so focused was an inspiration to me that ultimately helped lead to the idea for this book.) "Yeah, that's why I do it," he replies. "I think that's great."

Ludacris has even had the wherewithal to flip a negative situation into a positive one that helps others. Case in point: The infamous Bill O'Reilly incident.

In August of 2002, loudmouth Fox News commentator Bill O'Reilly hopped on his *O'Reilly Factor* program and called for a boycott of Pepsi Cola. He was steamed that it had chosen Ludacris to be one of its latest spokespeople.

"Ludacris spouts the usual antisocial nonsense that enthralls people like Elton John and apparently the executives that run Pepsi," declared O'Reilly, managing to sound both homophobic and racist in less than 20 words.

He later went on to add, "Obviously Pepsi could not care less about those children, because they're promoting a man that espouses violence, degrading sex, and substance abuse."

(A curious choice of words for a man whose novel, *Those Who Trespass*, has its share of violence and sex, but I digress.)

Within 24 hours, O'Reilly's call to boycott had generated so many telephone calls that Pepsi decided not to air the Ludacris ad that had already been filmed. And less than six months later, Pepsi ads featuring Ozzy Osbourne and two of his children, Jack and Kelly, began airing. Strangely, O'Reilly wasn't complaining about the Osbournes selling for Pepsi, though they'd probably even tell you themselves that they're not only more profane than Ludacris, but much more entrenched in the grip of substance abuse. Ozzy's battles and extreme relationship with drugs have of course been well documented over the years, while Jack and Kelly each took trips to rehab within two years of that commercial airing.

It was Russell Simmons who immediately stepped in to be at Ludacris' side and helped to turn the fiasco into something good. In exchange for allowing Pepsi to break the contract, the corporation entered into an agreement that they would work with the Ludacris Foundation to distribute money (reports vary from $1-$5million) to a mutually agreed upon list of charities.

Ludacris is certainly not the only artist in the South who performs community service. Others have stepped forward to make an incredible difference in peoples' lives. Mississippi's own David Banner is a graduate of Southern University with a Master's Degree in finance who parlayed his talent into a multi-million dollar recording deal with Columbia Records.

> 'the ludicris foundation is an organization that's geared to helping kids help themselves'

In 2003 and 2004 he held his first "Crank It Up" Scholarship Award contest with the release of his second album *MTA2: Baptized in Dirty Water*. Five people who found winning game pieces in their copies of Banner's album were each awarded $10,000 to put towards their secondary education (or that of a family member).

Four of the winners hailed from Southern towns, including a young man from Hendersonville, North Carolina serving a tour of duty as a soldier in Iraq. "I struggled to get my undergrad and then my Masters Degree and now that I have made it I am blessed with the ability to give back," says Banner in the winner's announcement.

Then there are businesses such as Atlanta's New Finish Construction, owned and operated by rapper T.I. and his uncle Quinton Morgan, which renovates houses in run-down neighborhoods and provides a higher standard of living to families living on Section 8 welfare.

T.I. wants to help correct some of the damage done to the communities by drug trafficking, a problem he admits he contributed to in the past. "The things that I've done," he says, in his record company biography, "it was basically a temporary solution to a permanent problem and some of those things may have caused harm, so whatever I can do to right my wrongs and take responsibility for my actions, I try to do. What I can do, I will do."

In New Orleans, Ronald 'Slim' Williams and Bryan 'Baby' Williams, proprietors of the Cash Money Records empire, are known for giving back to their community. Since 1999 they've hosted an annual Thanksgiving dinner, arming themselves with love and 2000 25-pound turkeys to share. Their Cash Money for Kids program treats academic stars in schools to tickets to Hornets basketball games, and their Johnny & Gladys Williams Foundation (named for their late parents) offers a range of gifts from food to scholarships.

They've even tried for several years to purchase the Magnolia Projects where they grew up and, meeting bureaucratic stalemate, have instead worked it out to cover rent for its sick and elderly tenants. There's also a more immediate form of assistance that Baby likes to throw down when he rolls through the town.

"I know what it is to not have anything and I can't stand to see people suffer like that, so, I go in my pocket and hand out $20 bills to the kids and $100 bills to the single moms," he told New Orleans music website *satchmo.com*.

Not to be discounted in this discussion are the many people who use their art as to heal and help uplift others. Sometimes this happens without the artist really realizing how much they are giving, while in other instances it's a lot more deliberate.

"I feel like the music is also community service," says Cee-Lo. "Because it's gonna affect some thinking. You will ultimately affect the action as well so music is the perfect medium and vehicle and tool to do so. And that's why even when I'm away it's almost as if I do missionary work when touring."

With the spotlight still firmly pointed at the Dirty South, look for more of these examples growing and flourishing under the heat. Whether it takes the form of food drives, scholarships or fulfilling the wishes of a terminally ill patient, the compassion of Southerners will shine through.

As stated in its website's mission statement, the Ludacris Foundation is built upon an eight-point plan called "The Principles of Success" to bring the following ideals to the lives of kids: Self-esteem, spirituality, communication, education, leadership, goal setting, physical activity and community service.

The site gives instructions on how non-profit organizations that focus on youth education may apply for a grant. Each year it also awards secondary school scholarships to graduating high school students.

Ultimately, Ludacris does not do this because he wants to be rewarded. But a little bit of positive recognition for his humanitarian achievements is always welcome, particularly when stacked up against some of the negative attention he has received from right-wing extremists.

So Ludacris more than deserves the honor he received from the City of Atlanta on June 7th, 2004: The key to the city and a proclamation of the day as Ludacris Foundation Day.

Take that, Bill O'Reilly.

AS POLITICAL AS THEY WANNA BE

FEATURING **Luther Campbell and Stat Quo**

"We no longer have a shepherd now/We're lost sheep/Have to open your eyes/You can't afford to sleep ..."
— *2 LIVE CREW, 'REVELATION'*

Yo – if BET is your CNN, I'm sorry to say that your shit's fucked up. For real.

It's a sad reality in America, though: Black Entertainment Television is the prime news source for millions of kids and young adults. To those unfamiliar with it, BET is the land where The Parkers are the First Family, Free (host of the daily video countdown show *106 and Park*) is Secretary of State and the swagger of 50 Cent's G Unit is the only defense force we need. It's where the major opinion program is called *Comic View*, and the term 'world affairs' refers to the sexual exploits of Jamaican dancehall kings like Elephant Man, Sean Paul and Beenie Man.

It's also where the really live video shit – I'm talking about that off-the-hook, seen nowhere else but on pay-per-view or your own damn bedroom shit – goes down after 3am on *UnCut*. Call that fair and balanced reporting?

Hang on though, that's not quite right to say. For one thing, that implies a perfect balance is happening on CNN, which is certainly untrue and to be left aside for the purposes of this particular discussion. Even a self-proclaimed "News Network" shouldn't be one's only source for information.

BET does run its own, albeit highly slanted, news program on weeknights, though it's not plugged on-air nearly as much as *106 and Park*. There's also the fact that *UnCut* is followed, way too close for comfort and too soon for most, by an inspirational hour, often hosted by the multiple speaking tongues of Texas televangelist Robert Tilton. That's about as sharp a contrast from UnCut's vibrating stripper booty as one could find on Earth. "I guess you've got to get 'prayed up' after watching it," Usher joked to the Associated Press.

Boom, there we have it. Balance. Right?

I'm breaking BET's metaphorical balls a bit here in order to illustrate something: There's not all that much in the way of educational programming (unless you're looking for anatomy lessons) to be found there.

It must be noted, however, that the network has actually made a real contribution to the national political dialogue, pretty much for the first time in nearly a quarter century of broadcasting. That's because it has become the main outlet for hip-hop artists to let people know about something more than their next album release date.

As David Banner explained to the *Jackson Free Press*, there aren't many other folks in America lining up to open this dialogue.

"People don't want to remedy black problems; they just want to control our communities," he says. "Honestly, if black kids, the entire urban community, are not on drugs or not in jail, they'll have more time to think about what's really going on. Not only that, we would have more voting power. The hate groups pushing zero tolerance see that if people are not on drugs, or convicted for crimes, then we will have power, voting power."

With a monumental presidential election hanging in the balance, 2004 was a year when hip-hop artists started to tap into their political power, realizing that they had much more impact on voters – particularly the young, elusive African-American ones – than did politicians. BET was the chief vehicle for this communication.

The daily video show *Rap City* occasionally had its Larry King moments, as host Big Tigger asked artists their views on voting and the election or when a rapper would fly loose with a topical thought while performing a freestyle in the show's booth. Far more people regularly tuned in to that program than the network's evening news, with viewers inhaling the messages more deeply.

The network was also home to some of the most effective campaign ads to be found on television. This mainly came from the group Break Bush Off, which used current music (such as The Roots' 'Break You Off') while dispensing facts particularly relevant to the African-American vote, including the devastating effects of the Dubya Administration.

African-American unemployment, homelessness and the number of people living in poverty all rose during the years 2000 to 2004..

"Bush has an agenda," they said, "but you are not a part of it."

99

Stat Quo: Trying to shine a light on reality.

Hip-hop even showed up at the 2004 Republican National Convention, when First Twin Daughter Jenna Bush referenced a certain pair of ATLiens in a somewhat misguided attempt to make her parents look hip to the young generation. "When we tell them we're going to see OutKast," she said, "they know it's a band and not a bunch of misfits." An unlikely place to see the Dirty South wielding power, to be sure, but also very indicative of its influence.

The name check was a "great tack," OutKast's Andre 3000 told *billboard.com*. "If you're on the team of the Republicans I think it was smart to do. 'Cos some people, they don't care. They're just like: Hey, I want to go to where all the cool people are."

Ironically, Andre 3000 was at the RNC, watching in the wings with a camera crew. At the behest of legendary television producer Norman Lear (*All in the Family*, *The Jeffersons*), he was interviewing people, including the Bush twins, for a documentary produced by Lear's non-partisan organization, Declare Yourself. And though Benjamin had been eligible to vote for more than 10 years, he said publicly that the 2004 presidential election would be the first where he would actually exercise his right.

> **2004 was a year when hip-hop artists started to tap into their political power**

Andre never felt like his vote was important before, blaming it both on being away from home all the time (no artist giving this excuse seems to have heard of an absentee ballot) and honestly feeling like it would make no difference for him to cast his opinion. He even questioned the vote on the song 'Git Up, Git Out' on OutKast's 1994 debut album, *Southernplayalisticcadillacmuzik*: "Y'all tellin' me that I need to get out and vote, huh? Why?/Ain't nobody black runnin' but crackers, so, why I got to register?"

Fortunately timed for when his celebrity status reached epic, nay, Gigantor proportions, Andre eventually came around to a different way of thinking, as many people have in the face of catastrophic world events. "If you don't vote, you're pretty much giving up your power," he said to *MTV.com*. "You're pretty much saying, 'Do what you will with me.'"

Andre also took in the Democratic National Convention, and, as he told MTV reporter Shaheem Reid, he finds some parallels between what he does and how politicians operate:

"Because I'm an entertainer, I know performance, I know showmanship, I know how to market certain things. I see a lot of that going on at these conventions. It's almost like a big concert, a big show; a lot of MCs going on one after each other, saying their rhymes, saying their punch lines, saying their key points, doing the little gestures and hand movements and getting the crowd amped. It's pretty much the same thing [as in rap]. They're selling something. They're trying to say, 'Get on my team or get down with my crew.' It is a big party. When they say 'political parties,' they mean that."

The presidential election provided a convenient excuse to get people thinking about their role in the political process. No one was trying to work miracles; getting people to simply vote was the goal. It almost seemed pre-emptive to work out what further work could be done given the heightened awareness among the hip-hop crowd. The danger of overwhelming people with too much substance was something to take into consideration. Now, the big question is, would people care to be political post-election? Time will tell how much does – or doesn't – stick with the people.

The events of 9/11 brought with them a dramatically modified sort of freedom for Americans. Civil liberties seemed to disappear with both alarming regularity and frightening alacrity, all in the name of increased national security. Atop a massive list of new restrictions in this country: Watch your damn mouth.

Many are taking heed of this new unfriendly attitude to free speech, with pretty good reason. The consequences are serious.

"A lot of artists are afraid," says Stat Quo, muting the Lil Flip video on his television and sitting up straight. "Because what the public doesn't understand is that our government, whether you wanna believe it or not, they understand the power of the mind. And if they feel that an artist is getting too political – every rapper has what you call a file. A fed file – every rapper has a federal file. The 'hip-hop police,' we call 'em. So when you do that kind of shit, certain bad things just tend to start happening to you. You start getting followed. It's a bad look. People don't understand that.

"But artists, the government definitely understands how powerful we are and they definitely monitor us. Believe me, if you've been on the radio and say, 'Don't vote for Bush. Bush is terrible for the country,' [etc], it's a wrap, you know what I'm saying? It's a wrap. They just opened your file and they start taking pictures of you and it's a bad look for you."

Stat Quo, for one, is emphatic: He's not going to let this sort of increased scrutiny muffle what he is ultimately trying to say in his music. As we saw in the chapter "On the Verge," Stat is at the critical point in his career where he's about to break out, where people will be looking at him to see what he has to say.

"I'm gonna do me," he says. "I'm gonna say what I wanna say. If you say it's free country, God dammit, let's go. I'm gonna act like I'm livin' in it. I'm gonna test it."

It's suggested to him that this is a lot of responsibility for a hip-hop artist right now.

"Yeah," he says, his gaze steady. "And I'm gon' tell it. We complain as a way to change what the fuck is happening. People are all, 'Well, you talkin' about gangsta rap, and …' Well, it's telling you what my fucking reality is. When I talk about certain shit, I'm telling you my reality, what I'm living in and then I'm letting you know, I'm basically reaching out for help. I'm trying to shine light on it, on what the fuck is going on, so it can change. And I definitely think hip-hop artists, a lot of people don't realize how powerful we are as far as making changes in the world. A lot of us are ignorant to that fact, that we affect so many people."

I mention to Stat that after I take care of a little more business in Atlanta I'll be heading down to Miami to speak to Luke Campbell, who, despite his reputation as a purveyor of sex-drenched entertainment, is one of hip-hop's most outspoken freedom fighters. "The things he went through made him understand how powerful it is," Stat replies. "Like I said, I think if I hadn't went through what I've seen personally with that – them taking pictures and shit like that – I think I wouldn't be the way I was.

"Luke went through a whole lot of shit with the freedom of speech [issue] and now every law student that goes through law school has to learn about that case. That was one of the biggest cases in US history. You know what I'm saying? They really was trying the freedom of speech."

Didn't go to law school personally, but I did study Luke's landmark 1990 case, Skyywalker Records v Navarro, while working on a Political Science degree.

"He's the reason why they put 'Parental Advisory' stickers on records," continues Stat. "People don't understand how significant that whole shit was … And people followed him around so much. And he was just talking about fuckin', you know? At the end of the day, that's what it is. You go to other countries, they fuck on regular TV!"

Miracle of miracles, even though graduation was just about 10 years ago, I still managed to find the highlighted text of the case (two, if you count his successful appeal) in a box of old papers. The first sentence of U.S. District Court Judge Jose Gonzalez' opinion in Skyywalker Records V. Navarro is priceless. "This," wrote Gonzalez, "is a case between two ancient enemies: Anything Goes and Enough Already."

Kinda funny to look back on that statement and think that it's almost 15 years later and people still have not had Enough Already. They're still having fun hitting Anything Goes from the back. Truth be told, since ye olden and quaint days of Skyywalker V. Navarro, shit has only gotten more UnCut.

" … We are bonded by the First Amendment. We have the freedom of expression. We have the freedom of choice. And you —Chinese, black, green, purple, Jew —you have the right to listen to whoever you want to, and even the 2 Live Crew. So all you right-wingers, left-wingers, bigots, Communists: There is a place for you in this world. Because this is the land of the free, the home of the brave. And 2 Live is what we are!"
2 LIVE CREW, 'Banned in the USA'

"My name is Luther," says Luke Campbell, hovering over a plate of Cuban chicken and rice. "So I always thought I was gonna be the next Martin Luther King."

It's kind of hard not to giggle a little when hearing this at first. In fact, I have to suppress the reflex that would have me squirt my banana shake out of my nose at the thought. No disrespect intended: It's only because the image of the late great leader stands at the opposite end of the spectrum from Uncle Luke, building his reputation as the black Larry Flynt with his adult DVDs. Uncle Luke has a dream: A wet one.

But it really isn't that silly after all. While their approaches couldn't be more different, there's certainly overlap when it comes to the intention of uplifting their people. Luther Campbell has constantly fought for the civil rights that Dr King set in motion, personally challenging the powers-that-be on the highest levels and encouraging anyone who hears him to be an activist.

Luke has been politically cognizant for as long as he can remember, he says. He was influenced by his Jamaican father and other Rastafarian relatives and friends who helped raise him. He was encouraged to keep his mind sharp from a young age.

"I used to stay with my uncle, who is dead now, God bless the dead," he recalls. "He told me old stories about him growing up, old hysterical black stories about him growing up, and he wouldn't let me look at cartoons when I'd go over there to stay with him on the weekends. And he let me know, 'I ain't letting you look at them cartoons. You better look at the news or they're gonna put them

> 'my name is luther, so i always thought i was going to be the next martin luther king'

chains back on your feet. You need to understand what's going on in the world today, but don't believe everything you read nor see.' So he really drilled it in me that I need to stay conscious of what's going on in the world."

Luke realizes that this sort of upbringing is definitely the exception in today's more politically apathetic climate. This being the case, he hopes that he is able to use his influence to guide people who may not be doing as much of their homework.

"Keep in mind a large portion of our people are into The Source, XXL and BET, so they ain't really paying attention to politics like everybody else is," he notes. "So I think it's important for them to have the confidence in people like myself and other people in those areas to say, 'Okay, you on some real shit. We know you gonna fight for what's right and if Luke say, "Yo, vote for this person right here" and we not keeping up with this shit here, I'mma take his word.' That's how I kinda look at it. And other people who do follow politics can make their choice. And I'm pretty sure the ones who follow [see] what I'm talking about …

"I think right now I feel like I have a responsibility of guiding my people in the right direction, you know what I'm saying? Like right now I be telling 'em to go vote for John

Luke Campbell: Guiding people in the right direction.

Kerry. I wouldn't have told 'em to go vote for Al Gore. Under no circumstance, because I had a problem voting for him because of the things me and his wife [music censorship cheerleader Tipper Gore] went through. If he was elected president and the things that Joe Lieberman tried to impose on hip-hop as well – I had a real problem going up in there sticking that."

A lot of artists told people to go out and vote in the 2004 presidential election, some of whom, as it turned out, weren't even registered themselves and had never voted in their lives. (For shame!) Luke's got a far better track record of electoral involvement, both in voting and in getting out the vote.

"For years I've been doing voter registration programs, going back about 10 years, getting people to vote, getting them cards and doing mobilization and that whole thing," he says.

This was all long before Florida became the most controversial state in the nation during the 2000 presidential election, when votes and results were 'mysteriously' tabulated incorrectly.

"I already knew Florida was gonna be the battleground state [in 2004], based on everything that was coming up. We knew it was gonna the case again this year. And now I got more time 'cos I'm not doing as much of the music thing as I was before. I'm more and more getting involved in the adult industry side of this business, trying to become the next Larry Flynt of urban adult entertainment, so I got a little bit more time while I'm cutting all these deals here to do that."

In fact, Luke becomes particularly active during every election, not just the one for president. To him, persuading others to be a part of the political process on the local level is the most important. That's where he sees the most potential for tangible results.

"I just wanted to spend a large part of this year just getting people to register and getting people to the polls in my backyard. I don't worry about the whole country too much, so what I did was I got with some politicians and they helped me out. [Florida Representative] Hank Harper and some other people, they helped me out.

"And what I figured was, if we could set up a model of how it should be around the country – I mean, you got all different people doing these voter registration drives but now you're getting them to get the card, now you gotta get 'em to vote. There's no model and there's no communication of a model that needs to be presented to our people, this hip-hop generation. So what I wanted to do is take my state, Florida, and come up with a plan of getting people registered to vote … Because from a national standpoint, the

> **a lot of artists told people to go out and vote in 2004 – some weren't even registered**

Bushes and all them or whoever, it trickles down to us. But the local shit is what you really have to deal with."

Luke touches on an issue that few in hip-hop appear to be thinking about, which is the importance of acting locally. He breaks down why it's vital to know what's going on in your own backyard.

"Here we got a mayor race, we got judges, we got police chiefs and sheriffs and all kind of shit we wanna deal with locally to determine how we live as a community and as people. Yeah, I mean, the national government and shit comes down, but then what happens to you on the ground floor? A lot of people get caught up with the presidential race. I say no, you need to be more focused on your local politics. Y'all go sift out the good politicians and the bad ones. You'll make changes. Like, for instance, in Daytona Beach: I don't think there was ever anybody on the commission black. Now Daytona got a black mayor and black councilmen, and all done through the black [voting body].

"So what I'm trying to do here is get people focused on local politics, deal with that so you can get more respect in the community because then that stops all the police harassment. That stops people continuing building projects and all that kind of stuff right there. Gives people more jobs and everything because the local government determines who gets the contracts to get jobs and who gets to beautify their community. All that stuff to the local government. The judges downtown when you feel like you're gonna get railroaded, you voted the judge in, you voted the state attorney in, you voted the mayor in. So you get respect in that sense where they don't fuck with you like that. So that's something that I wanted to do. You can see straight up results right there. So that's why I started it."

Luke expected to fulfill his goal of registering 40,000 new voters in Florida before the presidential election. Since the last election came down to just 537 votes in Florida, that's a more than significant number.

Part of Luke's political astuteness lies in his ability to glance into the mentality of the opposing side, and maybe even figure out its merits.

"The crazy part about it, right?" says Luke, leaning in over his plate of food for emphasis. "The crazy part about it is: I like [Bush]. Because he's real. That muhfucker real. I can relate to him. And that's the sick part about it. I sit up there and say, nah, I ain't gonna fuck with him. Because he real, he wear his shit on his – one thing in people I can't respect is people who talk out of one side of their mouth. Something they play that they're really not.

"This muhfucker arrogant and he wear his shit on his shoulders. He gon' tell you what he like and what he into and what he don't like and if you don't like it then fuck you. On the real. So that's what I like about him."

Despite his tremendous efforts in getting people to exercise their rights, Luke still falls pitfall to negative thinking sometimes, just like everybody else. After a somewhat somber discussion about U.S. foreign policy, we part ways feeling a just a little bit powerless. It's only normal. "We ain't nothing but pawns in the game," he sighs, knowing it's still time to fight the power anyway.

"I just don't ever want it to be said that I didn't try and make a difference as an individual," says Stat Quo. "Me, personally, if I didn't try and make a change I would be, like, shit. Like, damn, I had an opportunity to possibly stop it.

"But at the end of the day, Dre told me, 'Man, you gotta know that people don't wanna go to school.' People don't wanna feel like it's like your mom and dad talking to you. You gotta figure out a way to make it cool. You gotta give 'em what they want, and sprinkle what they need on top of it."

Stat cites Public Enemy's genius blend of serious reality (Chuck D) with energetic comic relief (Flavor Flav) as an example of a good balance at work. "They had Flavor Flav up there lookin' ignorant and sportin' the big clock and shit. It's like, 'Oh, shit!' And they made it cool."

Chuck D definitely wouldn't have had as much success in communicating his message to the average, everyday person were it not for Flavor Flav's antics backing him up. Public Enemy would not have been anywhere near as potent.

"No, it wouldn't have," he agrees, "because you gotta have that. You gotta have something where the motherfuckers, they just be like, 'Look at this motherfucker! He's up there, holy shit!' You gotta have that. If it's just like, 'Fight the power, fight the power' the whole way, and no Flavor Flav, it's not gon' work, you know what I'm saying? Flavor Flav was givin' 'em what they want. That's what he was doing. That's why he was so important to this shit.

"Like when he did the song '911 is a Joke.' People don't understand; that's some real shit. That's some real shit that was going on. But Flav made it to where it was, you know, 'Damn. This is the shit,' but he was sayin' something. Then you got into the message, like, 'That's real, man. 911 is a joke! They never come to my neighborhood!'"

Stat Quo is definitely no Flavor Flav, nor is he trying to be, but his point is well taken. It is still entertainment, in the end, so it should err on the lighter side. But entertainment shouldn't be a blindfold to what is happening in the world.

"Be more aware of what's going on," he advises. "I know local politics is boring. I know. But you gotta pay more close attention to what's going on."

Stat Quo looks up at his flat screen, which is now playing out the afternoon's headlines. He, like a normal man, watches BET of course. But not more than CNN: Oh no. Not a good look.

"Like, when the little things flash there across the bottom of the screen at one in the morning that don't flash at one in the afternoon or four in the afternoon? Read that! That's important right there. Just 'cos they're not saying it – read. You know what I'm saying?"

b-side

TEEMONEY'S DIRTY SOUTH AWARDS (TDSA)

Everyone likes a good awards show, so allow me to present the first annual edition of Teemoney's Dirty South Awards. Commercial free, no bullshit, fuck the red carpet, and Joan Rivers is most definitely not invited.

Unlike most award shows, you can't buy yourself a TDSA or ingratiate your way into getting one. Nope, this award comes right down to the incredibly biased opinions of one young woman. From San Francisco at that!

I can't afford to spring for the kind of prize I'd ideally like to give TDSA winners – mainly since I'm envisioning something fashioned out of rose gold and diamonds. And it was also too late to get the sexy trophy girls to stand behind the podium and greet the champions, since they needed 24 hours notice. (Who am I kidding? There's not even a podium!)

Instead I bestow on these TDSA recipients an undying amount of respect and blessings, for whatever it's all worth to them …

best side hustle
Winner: Chingo Bling

The *Houston Press* honored its hometown hero Chingo Bling with four of its Music Awards in 2004: Local Musician of the Year, Best Latin Rap, Best Local Label (for his Big Chile Enterprises) and Best New Act. We want to add Best Side Hustle to that list of accolades.

The rapper has a business degree and a champion cock – his pimp cup toting, prizefighting rooster Cleto, which is probably not what you were thinking – and is known for shedding light on the oppression of the Latino community with a gift of humor.

There are artists who began as drug dealers (or still maybe even moonlight as them), but Chingo Bling has instead made a lot of his money with a skillful blending of masa, pork shoulder and cumin, as he told *Murder Dog*.

"All the piece and chains, the toe wear, the ostriches, the custom Versaces with the Virgin Mary," says Bling, also known as the Tamale Kingpin. "You can't make all that off of CDs alone, you gotta have something else going on. Tamales is big business. I got that million dollar recipe ... If you look at rap music, that's all people talk about is slanging crack. They talk about cookin' this and that up, and that started in the '80s in New York and then it spread around, and all these conspiracy theories about Ronald Reagan, but Chingo was cooking up something else."

All that, and Chingo Bling also has a kind heart for those who might not be quite as talented as he when it comes to the music. He has even put out an open offer on his Web site.

"Rap isn't for everybody," he writes, "so put the mic down and come be one of my tamale wrappers."

rawest groupie scandal ever
Winner: Big Boi of OutKast

Mixtapes are the place to go to when you want to hear rappers feeling a degree less censored and offering material that will not make it to their album, whether it's lyrical beef being passed around by quarreling rappers or an exceptionally uncut story about life on the road. But there's still usually a limit to what is talked about.

Not on Atlanta DJ Drama's *Gangsta Grillz X* mixtape, though. OutKast's Big Boi, who hosts the whole set, talks about a scandalous evening many moons ago in a Chicago hotel room after a show. Amidst a session of large-scale sexual sharing, someone's valuable ring ended up disappearing. No one would admit to taking it, until ...

"Somebody came clean, went in her puss and pulled out a ring," says Big Boi. "That was the most gangster shit ever. I mean, *Gangsta Grillz!* Don't get no mo' gangster than that. That's the first time I ever seen a bitch put some gold and diamonds in her pussy, trying to walk out a hotel room with a nigga ring."

> 'rap isn't for everybody, so put the mic down and be one of my tamale wrappers'

man of the people award
Winner: Mike Jones

Who? Mike Jones! The successful independent rapper on the rise from Houston has been signed to the record label Swisha House since 2002, where he's sold hundreds of thousands of units, mainly in the South alone. As of this writing he's readying the release of two more albums which, paired with the video exposure he's gotten from BET's *UnCut* program for his 'Still Tippin' single and Swisha House's new major label distribution deal, should spell far more sales and national acclaim to come.

Just about every artist has a Web site; that isn't anything too remarkable in itself. Mike Jones happens to have a very cool site (*www.whomikejones.com*).

111

Houston rapper Chingo Bling with Cleto, his feathered friend.

Mike Jones: A true man of the people.

But no other artist, especially one of his stature, wants you to have his phone number. Mike Jones does. He even plasters it all over his T-shirts and mentions it often on records. Talk about a true man of the people.

Don't believe it? Call (281) 330-8004. And, uh, ask for Mike.

the lifetime achievement award for keeping speech free
Winner: Luther Campbell

"I just got my first award of any kind [in the music business] two weeks ago," Luke said during our interview in Miami. "Free Speech Coalition. I told them that and they almost fell out. I was like, 'Yo, thank you for the first award that I've ever received in the whole music industry, *period*.'"

So we want to piggyback on that award, Luke, and present your first Lifetime Achievement honor. At the time, we didn't understand the full political implications of fighting for the right to say, "Heeeeyyyyy, we want some pusssssssssssay!" But in this post 9/11 apocalypse, where freedoms are being snatched up every hour of every day, that victory is still crucial.

Especially since you took it and translated it into a credible force in the politics of your community and, by extension, the country.

the lifetime achievement award for keeping it too real
Winner: Bushwick Bill

Bushwick Bill set an impossibly high standard for keeping it too real back in 1991 when he flipped a traumatic incident into a memorable album cover for the Geto Boys' *We Can't Be Stopped*.

After demanding that his girlfriend shoot him and put him out of his misery, Bill was indeed shot, though not fatally – in his face. Who can forget that ultimate photo of him being rolled down the hospital corridor on the gurney with Willie D and Scarface, bloody bandage dangling off his eye?

We're not exactly encouraging people to try to top Bill's achievements, you understand. But in this age when everyone's trying to separate the authentic from the fake more than ever, just keep *We Can't Be Stopped* in mind. That's the original source of what Southerners now call *trill* – that's *triple real* for the rest of us. Bushwick Bill got that. He's one of America's first original reality stars.

Competition is already heating up for next year's Lifetime Achievement Award For Keeping It Too Real.

Word is that the committee wants to lighten up the festivities a bit next time around, though. So it might end up going to another one of Houston's finest, Devin The Dude,

115

for using a picture of himself smoking and reading the newspaper on the toilet for his 1998 debut album *The Dude*.

most promises in a can
Winner: CRUNK!!! Energy drink

Lil Jon had one of his alarmingly regular flashes of marketing brilliance when he called up a friend he had at a beverage distributor (a fellow I happened to meet on a flight to Texas a few months back) and said, "Crunk needs to be an energy drink."

Shortly later, the horny goat weed-and-guarana-fortified deliciousness known as CRUNK!!! was born, bearing the following promises on the can: "Invigorate," Arouse," "Energize," Replenish," "Stimulate," and "Refresh."

Oh, and "Get Your Crunk On!!"

At this point, I've got to go full disclosure and admit that, as a ridiculously caffeine-sensitive individual, I haven't actually tried CRUNK!!!, though one of its slick cans graces my desk (next to a can of Nelly's Pimpjuice). So whether the drink is actually able to make good on its promises is something that this committee has so far been unable to determine.

CRUNK!!! gets respect for putting forward a positive image overall, using their Web site to offer the sweetest definition of the word seen anywhere: "Taking the bad and finding the good and creating splendor out of the ugly is CRUNK!!! Recognizing each other as brothers and sisters is CRUNK!!! Upholding and taking care of family is CRUNK!!!"

Incidentally, we also hear that Lil Jon likes his CRUNK!!! mixed with Grey Goose vodka, something that is likely still swirling around in his pimp cup at various celebrity events.

oh how you slang those words award
Winner: B.G. for 'bling bling'

In 2003, the Oxford English Dictionary added a new term to its tome: 'bling bling.' First heard internationally via a 1999 record of the same name by B.G., it gives a name to the glimmer and gleam of fine jewelry such as platinum and diamonds and has come to be associated with the luxury lifestyle in general.

New Orleans rapper B.G. came to acclaim at a young age, and was a seminal part of the Cash Money Millionaires during their rise to prominence (both before and after Cash Money signed a $30m-plus deal with Universal).

He now has his own Chopper City Records and most recently released his second album since leaving Cash Money. (It's appropriately titled *Life After Cash Money*.)

During his career, B.G. has been plagued by many demons, most notably his public battles with drug addiction. But we honor him for a remarkable achievement in breaking

B.G.: King of 'bling bling.'

through to the mainstream consciousness, something few may claim. A dictionary is forever, baby.

"Bling bling will never be forgotten," B.G. tells *MTV.com*. "So it's like I will never be forgotten. I just wish that I'd trademarked it, so I'd never have to work again."

best babymaking vocals
Winner: Sleepy Brown

"I think that I'm bringing good, fun, soul music to the game, something for you to dance to," Brown tells *Atlanta Fever*. "I'm not trying to change the world."

Perhaps not. But the Dungeon Family member best known as one-third of the Organized Noize production crew (with Ray Murray and Rico Wade) and the beautifully buttery voice behind such hits as OutKast's 'I Like The Way (You Move)' and his own 'I Can't Wait' (featuring OutKast) is changing the world for the positive. We want to tip our hat to that with the honor of Best Babymaking Vocals.

> 'bling bling will never be forgotten, so it's like i will never be forgotten

Unfortunately, shifts and turns in the music business in 2004 meant that Sleepy Brown's highly anticipated album *For the Grown and Sexy* did not see its release when it was originally scheduled to drop in June. That probably meant a whole lot of babies that would not be born the following April, but watch for the boom once the album finally hits.

who you callin' a bitch award
Winner: Miss B

One of the highlights of my recent trip to Atlanta was learning about Miss B through her live performance at a showcase for the annual Atlantis Music Conference. Besides discovering that she's got both talent and charisma to take her far in this game, I also learned – and thankfully, not from personal experience – that she is not one to disrespect.

"I don't fight, I don't argue. I just hit that bitch with a bottle," she raps on the chorus of 'Bottle Action.' "Got problems? I'll solve 'em. I just hit that bitch with a bottle."

Might sound a little rough translated on paper, but Miss B managed to craft a perfect tune for any woman who needs an anthem to safely express some anger and bust some heads open, metaphorically of course. Jermaine Dupri must've agreed, picking up the track for a crunk compilation on So So Def. I know I can only sit here in anticipation that she might get to record a video for 'Bottle Action.'

An honorable mention must go to the fierce females of Atlanta's Crime Mob, Diamond and Princess. These young women are pretty much just getting started, but they wield intimidation tougher than nails on songs like their breakout hit 'Knuck If You Buck.'

best gangster infiltration into the mainstream
Winner: Baby for The Birdman shoe
You have to respect the marketing sensibility of Cash Money's Baby (aka The Birdman). He's one of several Southern moguls to parlay business knowledge originally honed from the wrong side of the law into solid legal money, but Baby may be one of the most brazen about it.

Take The Birdman, a "signature shoe" he designed in partnership with Lugz. For those unfamiliar with drug terminology, "bird" is a word for cocaine. Thus, what we essentially have is the coke shoe. Available at a mall near you!

Lugz is an urban company savvy to its market. They're not afraid to be less than subtle about this kind of theme, and we have to salute their balls for doing it.

"The sneaker features a clean-cut design," touts the corporate press release, "and each pair will include a special 'bling-bling' Cash Money Stack Clip (key chain for girls)."

Good thing, for a blinging clip is certainly a lot more sophisticated than a rubber band.

Initially priced at $70, The Birdman shoe is a lot more long lasting than, well, other things that someone could buy with that money.

wildest video shoot
Winner: T.I. for Birthday Bash promo
In the summer of 2004, self-proclaimed 'King of the South' T.I. was on a work release program from Georgia's Cobb County Jail (stemming from a violation of parole from a 1998 drug conviction). He had been serving time at nearby Fulton County since April.

In June, T.I. arranged to have a film crew come into Fulton County Jail to make a short video to preface his appearance at the annual Birthday Bash for Atlanta radio station Hot 107.9, the same show that would ignite a beef between the rapper and Houston's Lil Flip.

During the filming, prison inmate Cara Williams escaped from a processing area.

Although Williams was found and back in custody by the middle of that same night and, as *Associated Press* reports, she was the "10th escape or accidental release from the jail during the last 16 months," the incident must not have helped T.I.'s situation with Atlanta officials. It did, however, give the rapper the Wildest Video Shoot, and established a new meaning to 'Girls Gone Wild' in the process.

Atlanta rapper T.I., who styles himself 'King of the South,' knows how to work a crowd.

SPACE AGE PIMPING: 69+ WAYS TO GET DIRTY ON THE WEB

You don't have to be 18 and over to enter; this is a different kind of Dirty Web site directory. These selections represent a cross-section of what is available online, from artist and label sites (both official and unauthorized) and regional communities to more general hip-hop sites in which Southern issues may only be one component.

With artist websites, it's always interesting to see who has taken the time to make sure their site is tight and, on the other hand, who might not even know they have a website! Also fun is to check who owns their own domain names or what distinctly non-Dirty South things reside at the *dotcom* address of your favorite artist. The results could make for a pretty funny collection of stories. Obviously people are interested in computers and technology to varying degrees, but plenty of folks have truly tapped into the potential of the medium to offer visitors a worthwhile destination experience.

And then there are the everyday fans that love Dirty South music and culture. They may be found online, posting in forums and discussions and meeting each other on sites like *Memphis Rap* and *Dirty South Rap.*

It goes without saying that there are more ways to Get Dirty on the Web to be found in this book than just these (though you might notice that I've slipped in a few more than 69 here in between the lines).

But these sites will provide a gateway/hub to discover many of the new, relevant sites that are constantly launching in cyberspace. Additionally, many of the publications listed in the Media Center have excellent Web sites (URLs are provided in that chapter).

2-4-1 Records
http://www.241records.com
This South Florida label is a collaboration between legendary DJ crews Jam Pony Express and Bass Style DJs. The former are legends that *Ozone* writer Felisha Foxx calls "Florida's best-kept secret for two decades" and credits with coming up with popular party chants like "To the window, to the wall" and "Hold up, wait a minute, let me put some bass in it."

Today their focus is on their production arm, the Hit Droppaz, and developing artists such as Supa Star Rated R, Eve'nin Ridahz and Da' Diamond – all projects described in further detail on their Web site.

All Hip-Hop
http://www.allhiphop.com

Billed as "the world's most dangerous site," *All Hip-Hop* is the online destination of choice for hip-hop music lovers, industry gossips and even law enforcement trying to bone up on current beefs.

It is definitely my favorite hip-hop site on the Web, hands down, generating something in me that hangs on the cusp of addiction. A combination of solidly reported news items, in-depth interviews, new and exclusive songs (from mixtapes and upcoming albums) and truly juicy rumors, keeps people coming back.

It's not unusual for it to be updated a few times in one day, which, be forewarned, can make it hard to get work done! If you can't stand to be away from *All Hip-Hop* when not at your computer, they'll deliver news and updates to your cell phone or pager.

All Music Guide
http://www.allmusic.com

All Music Guide is the place to go for those who want to know some of the technical details of their favorite artists, from bios and discographies to Grammy Awards and *Billboard* chart placements. A vast resource for most types of popular music, with a fairly comprehensive look at a great many Southern hip-hop artists. My patient and understanding publisher Backbeat Books puts out various *All-Music Guides* as thick, encyclopedic volumes for those who prefer a ready reference to put on the bookshelf, while the Web site is constantly updated to reflect new artists, releases and noteworthy incidents in the history of music.

Ballaz Inc.
http://ballazinc.com

Looking for playalistic buddy icons for AOL or simply to find updates on the moves of the moguls? The Ballaz got you.

Ballerstatus
http://www.ballerstatus.net

While providing news and interviews from throughout the rap world, *Ballerstatus* (which began in 2002) seems to have a soft spot for the South and the West Coast.

While not updated as frequently as a site like *All Hip-Hop*, it still is home to some interesting feature stories. Best of all, the site offers free email accounts so you can get your pimp on with a *ballerstatus.net* address.

Big Tyme Recordz
http://bigtymerecordz.com

The Houston independent record label was the first home to UGK's Bun B and Pimp C and also released early works from DJ Screw. Nowadays the label continues to look at music from a screwed perspective.

Bone Crusher
http://www.bonecrusherfightmusic.com

This site was set up to promote big Bone's anticipated sophomore album *Fight Music* and offers a place to check out his latest videos and singles online. It is a branch off of the So So Def site (http://www.soso-def.com) which provides updates about Bone alongside labelmates such as Anthony Hamilton and J-Kwon. Perhaps Bone's own label Vainglorious will pop up online soon.

Bubba Sparxxx
http://www.bubbasparxxx.com

Bubba Sparxxx is an artist who has worked with the likes of Timbaland and Organized Noize and is presently working on his third full-length album. His site offers a fairly standard format with news, tour dates, photo gallery and a forum.

What would make this site truly take off is if Bubba were to interject some personal views from his unique perspective as a white rapper from the backwoods of Georgia who's made it into the echelons of Dirty South music by trying to illustrate rural life. For instance, it would be great to know more about the vision he has for his generation and beyond, known as the New South.

"To me the New South is just all about dispelling negative stereotypes associated with the South while acknowledging that most stereotypes exist for a reason, because in a lot of instances that is the case," he told British magazine *Blag*. "By no means is the New South a reality; it's very much still a vision for the future. We've come a long way in the past 20 or 30 years here in the South, that's how people perceive it in terms of race relations, in terms of poor education … But we've taken great strides. What goes on in the South today is still a reflection of what went on in the South 150 years ago. So, what we do today, the changes we make right now, will determine how people live in the South 150 years from now."

Cash Money Records
http://www.cashmoney-records.com

The official Cash Money Records site has all the polish and normal features of a major label Web site, with a few notable touches that make it stand out. One is their game section, where users can play games like *Concentration*, *Rock Tha House* and, most impressively, the 3-D rendered *Bling Buggies*. They also offer extras like cartoon trading cards, e-cards to send to friends, AOL buddy icons and wallpapers. Also worth checking is Cash Money's section of the impressive Louisiana music site *Satchmo* (http://www.satchmo.com/cashmoney), which has bulletin boards dedicated to the label and also to New Orleans rap as a whole, alongside Cash Money news, press releases and artist bios.

Cee-Lo
http://www.ceelo.net
Cee-Lo's current incarnation of his official site features our hero as a majestic yet somewhat menacing cartoon. While this might change as future projects materialize, the regular features of bio, tour dates, news and lyrics will probably stay intact.

Certified Crunkness
http://www.certifiedcrunkness.com
Hosted by Atlanta promoters Botchey & Zae Entertainment, *Certified Crunkness* announces their current club events and parties but also provides a message board for the local crunk community.

Chamillionaire
http://www.chamillionaire.com
Click inside for Chamillionaire Radio, Chamillionaire TV, contests with really good prizes and all the info you seek about this Houston rapper. But he's also got plenty of info on such all-star colleagues as Michael '5000' Watts, Lil Flip, Mike Jones and Slim Thug.

Chingo Bling
http://www.chingobling.com
Online home of the Tamale Kingpin and his label Big Chile Records features heavy input from the artist himself alongside audio downloads, video clips, tour dates, and more.

There's a merchandise area, so you can be the first on the block to get an Air Chingo T-shirt or a copy of one of many albums, like *Chingo Bling is Gone Off That Lou Diamond Syrup*. Perhaps most exciting is how ladies can sign up to be the next "Chingo Bling Bideo Gurl." Girls, warm up your Stupid Butt Tricks!

Crooked Lettaz
http://www.crookedlettaz.com
David Banner and his crew that make up b.i.G.f.a.c.e. Entertainment rest their online hats here, with a framework to provide photos, audio and information about upcoming

albums and tours. Not too much up here at the time of writing, but the potential's there.

Crunk Mansion

http://www.crunk-mansion.de

One of the Dirty South's most dedicated fan bases outside of the American South resides in Germany, perhaps a natural extension of their love of the gangstafied beats, bass and car culture of the West Coast.

Crunk Mansion, alongside another German site called *Third Coast*, provide some of the most updated information around. Those of us whose German is a little rusty can always paste bits of the text into an online translator such as Babel Fish Translation (http://world.altavista.com).

David Banner

http://www.david-banner.com

David Banner's official solo site offers several standard features (an archive of audio and video, message board, news, photos).

If I were to drop a suggestion in his comment box, I'd love to know about the progress of the five winners of Banner's scholarship contest: Where are they going to school? What do they want to study? And how has Banner's generous gift made the difference in their lives?

Devin The Dude

http://www.herecomesthedude.com

Devin's space is under construction at the moment, but knowing his sense of humor, I'm gonna make an exception for a site unseen and go out on a limb to guess that you can probably expect a couple of offbeat features to show up after the groundbreaking. If not, I'm gonna have to go to Houston and demand an explanation. Don't let us down, Dude.

The Dirty Dirty South

http://groups.msn.com/TheDirtyDirtySouth

This Dirty South interest group is one of hundreds, or probably thousands, of groups available to join on *msn.com*. While there is a discussion component to the group, there seems to be a stronger emphasis on hooking up users with other users.

The Dirty South Dot Com

http://www.thedirtysouth.com

Part of a network of online destinations from Planet Hip-Hop (http://planet-hiphop.com), this site has a little bit of this and a little bit of that, from videos, live clips and video interviews to feature stories and links.

Dirty South Radio
http://www.dirtysouthradio.com

Streaming Internet radio from Central Florida brings an upfront pirate radio feel to your computer. Tune in for live sets from DJs such as White Dawg, White Boi Pizal, DJ Baby Lac and DJ Hollywood in addition to special guests. Its charts section allows users to check the last 10 songs played in addition to joints in heavy rotation.

Dirty South Rap
http://www.dirtysouthrap.com

DSR features lots of contests, a teeming forum with a lot of members, the occasional news item and an archive of interviews with artists like T.I., South Park Mexican and Ludacris. Not the most timely updating happening here, but a good spot for general information nonetheless. Most of the action is happening in the section called "Hot Boys & Girls," which allows people to rate others based on hotness. On their scale, 10 is "flawless," 6 is "bangable," 3 is a "double-bagger" and 1 is "hideous."

Dirty South Web Ring
http://home.flash.net/~rob24/dirtysouth

Its name is somewhat false advertising, for this Web ring seems to include lots of broad hip-hop sites that don't appear to be Southern in origin. But I include this one for the sheer randomness of what might end up here, if you're feeling adventurous. Most listed here are fan-based and homemade, but comb these sites for surprises, including new music and artists.

Dope House Records
http://www.dopehouserecords.com

Houston artist South Park Mexican and his brother created Dope House Records, a successful label that not only releases SPM albums (he's now on his ninth) but nurtures the careers of artists like Baby Beesh, Juan Gotti and Lucky Luciano. Expected features are all here, with the additions of a section called "Ask Los" where fans can get answers straight from the South Park Mexican himself. Entrepreneurial spirits can learn how to join the Dope House team by repping the label or even setting up a Dope House store in their neck of the woods. Pay's not bad, either ... sheeit, if I lived in an area they were targeting I might just have to look into a franchise.

Down-South
http://www.down-south.com

When I first started this book I was excited to have the use of *Down-South* at my disposal. Its extensive archive, with many in-depth interviews conducted by the

Godfather of Dirty South history and criticism, Charlie Braxton, would surely be an indispensable research tool. Unfortunately, *Down-South* took a holiday for a face-lift during these last few months, so I couldn't reference anything. But given that it was the type of kick-ass site that didn't need improvement to begin with, its next incarnation is sure to be something special.

Get Crunk!
http://www.get-crunk.com

This (not-so) thoughtful translator allows users to type in whatever they would like translated into crunked-out Lil Jon speak. Unfortunately, they misspell our buddy's name and, without totally giving it away, this is basically a two-trick pony. Hopefully they'll take a cue from the famous Snoop Shizzolator and expand their word possibilities; if they wanna keep up they'll also have to build a mechanism to translate any Web site into Lil Jon poetics. This is pretty lousy, but it's funny that someone came up with it.

Grand Hustle Entertainment
http://www.grandhustle.com

Atlanta's T.I. is at the forefront of Grand Hustle, which also has a stable comprised of artists such as P.$.C., Xtaci, Big Kuntry and Mackboney & AK. What's most striking about this site is that T.I. doesn't dominate the space here, instead keeping somewhat equal billing with his colleagues. No ego trips here.

Houston Hip-Hop
http://www.houstonhiphop.com

This community-based destination keeps its structure short and sweet, with sections for a forum, user-contributed reviews and event listings.

Hypnotize Minds/Three 6 Mafia
http://www.triplesix.com

Many unofficial sites float out there, yet the authorized site for Hypnotize Minds and Three 6 Mafia provides a broad overview and history of this camp's work. They even have a "Beat Shop," where, if your budget's right, you can hire the skilled HM producers.

Lil Jon & The East Side Boyz
http://www.liljononline.com

The King of Crunk provides needed tools for crunk living: Previews of the latest Lil Jon & The East Side Boyz songs and videos, e-cards, wallpaper, ringtones and more. Also a hub that links visitors to the latest Lil Jon business endeavors (like CRUNK!!! energy drink and his Oakley Zero sunglasses).

Lil Troy
http://www.liltroy.com

Houston's Lil Troy and his label Short Stop Records lives here. It features fan club and artist info, a chat room, tour dates, audio/video and a shop. You can also catch behind-the-scenes looks at videos as well as lyrics and photos.

Louisiana Music Artist Directory
http://www.satchmo.com/nolavl/noladir.html

Curious about C-Murder, Mystikal, Funky Meters or the Neville Brothers? They're all catalogued in one spot, part of a larger mega-site dedicated to the music history of Louisiana and New Orleans. It feels good to see the hip-hop get as much reverence as the jazz at Satchmo, which honors the late Soulja Slim as much as any other notable musician who has passed.

Ludacris
http://www.ludacris.net

Luda's official site changes according to the album project he's working on. For his next album *Red Light District* he'll likely vary the presentation from the cute animated sequences that are a highlight of his *Chicken N Beer*-themed site. Look for the continuation of LudaTV, likely to be just that much racier with the theme of *Red Light District*. And don't forget his site for his non-profit organization, The Ludacris Foundation (http://www.theludacrisfoundation.org), which explains its mission.

DJ Magic Mike
http://www.djmagicmike.com

The bass master himself, Orlando's DJ Magic Mike, hosts his own site, providing info for upcoming events along with a discography, bio and media section. His space was mostly under construction at the time of viewing.

Maggotron/DXJ
http://www.maggotron.com

Dedicated to the Miami bass and electro experiments of Maggotron and DXJ as well as the label Jamron Records (which also has a separate URL at http://www.jamronrecords.com), this site is run by DXJ himself. He provides both history and updates as to current projects and also offers a rare shot at purchasing classic material from his archive without having to hit up eBay and pay extortionate prices.

Memphis Rap
http://www.memphisrap.com

Memphis boasts a thriving online community with dozens of features, so many that it can boggle the eye when trying to absorb it all. There's a very active community based on forums and member interaction, a deep archive of interviews of artists big and small, the latest sound and video clips, lyrics, local radio guide, fan club directory and tons more. Those seeking a primer on the music from Memphis couldn't find a more extensive place to go.

305/Miami Hip Hop
http://www.305hiphop.com

Miami Hip-Hop rivals *Memphis Rap* for providing a relevant and well-maintained space for their respective communities. Magazine-style features and editorials sit alongside areas for MC battles, discussions, video games and new music information. There's yet another set of forums at rival site *The305* (http://www.the305.com) if you're looking for more Miami.

Mike Jones
http://www.whomikejones.com

True, it's not as immediate as hollering at Mike Jones on his cell phone (the number is included on the site for those who would prefer to do that). But Jones has a decent Web site, with a sleek interface that allows for smooth paging through sections such as the ones set up for streaming audio and video, merchandise and news.

My Block
http://wordofsouth.com/myblock

This forum dedicated to Dirty South music and culture attracted 800 members in its first two months after beginning in the summer of 2004. Participants may discuss a range of topics, from critiquing albums ("Under Review") and current affairs ("Higher Intellect") to plain old shit talking ("Moufin' Off").

Nappy Roots
http://www.nappyroots.com

The dynamic group Nappy Roots has an appropriately vibrant site with the expected offerings of music samples, news and tours. They actually pop in and drop off messages and interact with fans. Others have been known to do that but is still a rare enough occurrence on artist sites.

The New No Limit Records
http://www.thenewnolimit.com

The New No Limit Records is now an inter-generational label, thanks to two generations of Master P's family on the roster: P and his brother Silkk the Shocker and P's son, the teen heartthrob Lil Romeo. Album previews are probably the highlight of this otherwise standard site, typically offering sound samples for each song.

Nobody Smiling
http://www.nobodysmiling.com

A general interest site for hip-hop music at large, *Nobody Smiling* is a respected source for news and updates. Print and radio interviews, games, wallpaper and bulletin boards provide bonus distractions, as do plenty of audio previews of new songs by top artists.

North & South Carolina Hip-Hop
http://www.stinkzone.com/carolinas/html/index.php

Carolinas! C'mon and raise up … sorry, you've probably heard that one before. Stop by here for a comprehensive radio guide, community discussions and the latest on established and up and coming artists. With artists as diverse as Little Brother, Twip and Petey Pablo already out in the national consciousness, imagine just how much more talent is lurking in these states, ready to go.

The Original Hip-Hop Lyrics Archive
http://www.ohhla.com

OHHLA has long been my site of choice when looking up hip-hop lyrics for reference. That's not to say it is 100 per cent accurate (though it definitely asks for help in correcting mistakes and updates songs accordingly). But its archive of artists and convenient cross-reference format makes research simple. And no one can beat the innovative little feature called the Rhymerator for originality. This multi-faceted section enables users to find rhyming words and suggestions for metaphors based on words. There's an established MC on hand to provide assistance if needed, even visuals to get the creative juices flowing. Dope.

OutKast
http://www.outkast.com

For the release of the dynamic duo's double album *Speakerboxxx/The Love Below*, La Face Records created a clever split site for each record to express the different personalities of Andre 3000 and Big Boi. As the site morphs into the identity of their next project, expect the same level of quality access to video downloads, bios, news and tour dates. Doubtless, some new surprises await.

Patchwerk Recording Studio
http://www.patchwerk.com

Any number of classic albums has been recorded at Patchwerk in Atlanta, and it remains a hub of activity for superstars as well as hot new artists. The studio has one of the more extensive sites for a recording studio. Beyond the facility to book time and care directly at Patchwerk, there are artist spotlights, forums to discuss production and a "tip of the month" for aspiring producers.

Peaches Records and Tapes
http://www.peachesrecordsandtapes.com
Those outside the vicinity of New Orleans could not ask for a more enlightening source for local rap music than Peaches Records and Tapes. Extensive sound samples minimize risk-taking when buying music – we're talking snippets of whole albums. Peaches boasts several specialties, so if some New Orleans gospel, blues or brass bands are needed, they can take care of that, too.

Pitfall Kennels
http://www.pitfallkennels.com
"Home of the rare blue pit," Pitfall Kennels is a trusted pit bull breeder owned by OutKast's Big Boi. I'm not sure if this is an industry standard, but Pitfall is able to deliver the puppy you pick from pictures online right to your door. Not only that, but they might even be sired by a male pit named Blue Pac or Supa Snoop. How hip-hop is that?

Playahata
http://www.playahata.com
A most unique general hip-hop site, *Playahata* offers satires (almost in the style of brilliant humor paper *The Onion*) to lighten up the mood. It's sometimes necessary comic relief in the midst of their raw and relentless reviews (books, films and records), gossip and interviews with hip-hop intellectuals who assume various roles within the culture. It's a place where blunt honesty is not only appreciated, it is expected.

Rap-A-Lot Records
http://www.rapalotrecords.com
Rap-A-Lot 4 Life! One of the original Southern heavyweight labels, home to the Geto Boys and Scarface as well as Devin the Dude, Juvenile's UTP, Dirty and others. The site presents the latest videos and products for sale and has one of the more useful online forums for a record label.

The Screw Shop
http://www.thescrewshop.com
They call it "the best place to get screwed," and besides DJ Screw's official Screwed Up

Records, they are probably right. Taking a cue from *The Source*, they have a section called "Unsigned Hype," and they also list new albums of which to be aware. By talking about and drawing attention to new releases even outside of the ones they sell, *The Screw Shop* makes a statement about supporting music. Their list of Dirty South related links is well-rounded and categorized. And if you're in Austin, you can visit their actual physical shop on Far West Boulevard.

Screwed Up Records

http://www.screweduprecords.com

The passing of Houston's Robert Davis Jr (aka DJ Screw) in 2000 was devastating to the crew and fans of this DJ who pioneered a signature style of manipulating records. The thriving "screw" culture has only gained momentum since his death, and his cottage industry built up from his frequent mixtapes continues on. Choose from dozens of original Screw tapes an CDs and understand the foundation of an enduring legacy.

Slim Thug

http://www.slimthugthaboss.com

Another of Houston's heroes, Slim Thug, has a damn near 3-D site. Either that, or it's just some clever graphical trickery that makes pictures pop out with extra sparkle. Prior to the launch of his *Already Platinum* album, the site mainly contained a video collection and the latest news.

Slow Motion 4 Me

http://www.slowmotion4me.com

This large community dedicates itself to the education and preservation of screw music, from its origins with DJ Screw to the current efforts from labels like Swisha House. The highlight is the audio section, which brings out chopped and screwed remixes of all sorts of songs. You haven't lived until you've heard D'Angelo screwed.

DJ Smallz

http://www.djsmallz.com

Florida's DJ Smallz is a Dirty South entrepreneur, offering marketing services, DVDs and acclaimed mixtapes like his *Southern Smoke* series, featuring big name hosts. He's currently developing a television show, Southern Smoke TV, and operates a weekly Sirius Satellite Radio show, Southern Smoke Radio (http://www.southernsmokeradio.com).

Sound of Hip-Hop

http://www.sohh.com

SOHH may be the biggest competition that *All Hip-Hop* has when it comes to a general site. Frequently updated news, artist pages, bulletin boards, chat rooms, interviews, audio/video and all that good stuff abound, as do history, battle analyses and gossip.

Southern Entertainment Awards
http://www.southernentawards.com

If Teemoney's Dirty South Awards weren't enough (how dare you?), here's a legitimate awards show serving the South. SEA not only honors artists and producers but mixtape and radio DJs, nightclubs and even gentlemen's clubs!

Southern Rap on Download.com
http://music.download.com/3605-8541_32-0.html

For those who want to dig for new and unreleased music from up and coming Dirty South artists, this free MP3 download site is a solid place to go. Optimists will feel it just might provide early warning of places like Pine Bluff, Arkansas, or Somerset, Kentucky, as future hotbeds of this music on a national scale.

Southwest Connection
http://www.southwest-connection.com

Subtitled "Third & West Coasts Collide," Southwest Connection provides an online outlet for the natural synergy between the South and California, with content ranging from movie and music coverage to forums and shopping.

Swisha House
http://www.swishahouse.com

Swisha House Records from Houston has an eye-popping site that was obviously crafted with a lot of care, which is not surprising given their commitment to releasing quality music. Jam-packed with photos, videos, music, news and more.

Tampa Hip-Hop
http://www.tampahiphop.com

Music and artist information is at the heart of *Tampa Hip-Hop*; downloads of "hot music" are the first elements you see when logging on. There's an extensive section for several dozen artists and DJs powering the scene as well as event listings, links, message boards and a store.

Texas Hip-Hop
http://www.texashiphop.com

This is mainly a member-based forum to discuss the Texas rap scene. There are areas to discuss politics, share event information and general issues.

Third Coast
http://www.third-coast.de

Once again, Germany displays its love for the Dirty with a Web site that is so extensive, it makes one wish for an American counterpart that is as organized and timely. It's a small world after all.

Timbaland Heaven
http://www.timbalandheaven.com

This may be an unofficial fan site for super-producer Timbaland but it has a lot to see. Among its highlights are a fairly informative list of various productions and remixes, an archive of news and items of note, and lots of resources for Tim's fans to meet each other. It also reveals several fun facts like his favorite cereal (Frosted Flakes, apparently).

TJ's DJs
http://www.tjsdjs.com

TJ Chapman's legendary DJ record pool based in Tallahassee, Florida has been an instrumental force in helping break records in the Southeast in its decade of existence. Check their charts for an indication of the hottest club and radio bangers. If you can find their hidden page of new MP3s, you're in for a treat.

Trina
http://www.trina-online.com

Trina's no exception to the typical artist site with news, tour dates and so forth. But, to answer the question that most guys will have: Yes, there are lots of photos of Trina.

TR-808
http://www.tr-808.com

At the source of all bass-heavy Southern hip-hop music is the classic Roland TR-808 Rhythm Composer, the wonderfully versatile drum machine that made bounce bounce, crunk get crunk and speakers go boom. This site gives the 808 the glory and reverence it deserves, with heaps of technical specifications and modifications, samples, links and discussion. The online electronic music resource *Hyperreal* has also got a loving 808 tribute with a lot of valuable info(http://machines.hyperreal.org/manufacturers/Roland/TR-808).

UGK
http://www.geocities.com/countryraptunes

Another fan-driven site, this one dedicated to the Underground Kingz, Pimp C and Bun B. Their record label offers only a small shell of info about UGK (which will probably only change as they have a new product to promote), but this spot has a full bio plus lyrics.

Ying Yang Twins
http://www.yingyangmusic.com
D-Roc and Kaine might be some of the hardest working entertainers. The duo are constantly on the move and need a constantly updated site to reflect their comings and goings, which they fortunately have here. Kaine mentioned in our interview that they pretty much haven't had a vacation since becoming the Ying Yang Twins in 1998, and if he ever had the chance to have one, he'd seek a moment of isolation. "I'd probably just go lay in the woods," he reckons. "Lay in the woods like muhfuckers. Go perform to some snakes and shit. I perform for all of these people, got dammit, go perform for some snakes and wolves."

Young Buck
http://www.young-buck.com
Buck's catchy site makes good use of image manipulation and pop-up action and offers a selection of mixed media as well as a big collection of desktop wallpaper and buddy icons for AOL.

THE SINGLES CLUB

Those who know DJs know that many of us like to make charts of favorite songs. Behold some very personal and slightly unusual top 10s (assembled in alphabetical order). They collectively form a whole mega-mixtape on their own, an eight-sided hardcore smackdown of memorable tunes.

LADIES FIRST:

Ciara featuring Missy Elliott: '1,2 Step'
Jazze Pha constructs a lively and infectious electro groove (think Afrika Bambaataa and Kraftwerk) for the young R&B singer's second single. And a little sprinkle of Missy is always good.

Chyna Whyte: 'What They Want'

For the Crunk and Disorderly compilation, Chyna looks at life from the perspective of a female mack.

Gangsta Boo: 'Where Dem Dollas At'

Prior to being saved and briefly changing her moniker to Lady Boo, the former Three 6 Mafia queen pen offered a sonnet for strippers and civilian women in hot pursuit of a man's money.

Jacki-O: 'Slow Down'

This Timbaland-produced track is the perfect follow-up to Jacki's sensationalist 'P°°°y (Real Good),' which flexes her lyrical skills in a deliberately less sexual way.

Khia: 'My Neck, My Back'

With the most thorough cunnilingus instructional ever to appear on record, Khia makes sure that all the angles are covered. The song also inspired a particularly brilliant answer record in the form of Too $hort's 'My Dick, My Sack.'

Mia X: 'Payback II'

Channeling the sharp tongue of ballsy black comediennes like Ms. Millie Jackson, former No Limit Records first lady Mia X has scathing words for her opposition.

Miss B: 'Bottle Action'

From the Bankhead area of Atlanta comes an irrepressible anthem about what will happen to the hapless bitches that try to test Miss B's patience in the club (poor dears).

Missy Elliott: 'Work It'

With its clever backwards hook (which is fun to play backwards in the mix to reveal what exactly it is she's saying) and brazen, sassy lyrics, Missy worked this song till the cows came home. And then worked it some more.

Rasheeda: 'Vibrate'

The original version of this hyperactive tune from Atlanta's 'Queen of Crunk' was so hot, enticing the strip clubs with its directives ("shake that shit till you start an earthquake"), Petey Pablo snatched it up and hopped on a new version with her for his second album.

Trina: 'Pull Over'

"I got a fat ass and I know how to tote it," raps the Miami mami. Trina earned my tongue-in-cheek respect forever for performing an unapologetic ode to her ample backside – which, even after many years and despite her best efforts, still gets more attention than anything else.

SOUTH/WEST COAST COLLABORATIONS:

Dr. Dre featuring Devin The Dude and Snoop Dogg: 'F°°° You'

A popular album cut from Dre's Chronic 2001 introduces Houston's talented Devin to international ears who might not have heard his work with the Geto Boys and the Rap-A-Lot label. When it comes to getting with females, Devin and Snoop figure that honesty is the best policy. Croons Devin, "I just wanna fuck you/No touchin' and rubbin', girl/You got a husband who loves you/Don't need you all in mine …"

E-40 featuring 8Ball: 'Ya Blind'

Brothers from another mother, the Bay Area's E-40 and 8Ball of Memphis join forces to provide further evidence that gangsters and pimps don't dance, they boogie – in this case, when Jazze Pha sings on the hook.

E-40 featuring Lil Jon & the East Side Boyz, Bone Crusher and David Banner: 'Anybody Can Get It'

Before their respective major label debuts, Bone and Banner turned in high-energy performances for 40, who in turn has no trouble matching their crunkness.

Lil Jon & the East Side Boyz featuring E-40, Petey Pablo, Bun B & 8Ball: 'Rep Yo City'

From the double-platinum *Kings of Crunk* album, a song to do Atlanta, Vallejo, the whole state of North Carolina, Houston and Memphis proud.

Lil Jon & the East Side Boyz featuring Nate Dogg, Snoop Dogg, Suga Free and Oobie: 'Bitches Ain't Shit'

Lil Jon brings out female singer Oobie, his secret R&B weapon, as an ideal counterpoint to Nate Dogg's singing, while Snoop and cohort Suga Free kick some pimp logic.

Miss B: Broke through with 'Bottle Action.'

Ludacris featuring Nate Dogg: 'Area Codes'

The runaway hit from the *Rush Hour 2* soundtrack will forever reign as a classic
player's anthem that finds both Luda and Nate in absolute top form. Everyone needs
hoes in different area codes – how good of them to remind people.

Nate Dogg featuring Ludacris: 'Real Pimp'

In this post-script to 'Area Codes,' Nate still sounds smooth as ever and Luda never
runs out of analogies for his ladykiller skills: 'Ever since Ruffles had ridges/Luda had
bitches.'

Scarface featuring 2Pac: 'Smile For Me Now'

Dozens of posthumous Tupac Shakur collaborations have been recorded since his
untimely death in 1996, but this early one remains one of the very best. It's both
gorgeous and truly heartbreaking, as Scarface, acknowledged to be a heavy influence
on Pac as a rapper, pays tribute to the thug angel who in turn affected him so deeply.

Snoop Dogg featuring Pharrell and Uncle Charlie Wilson: 'Beautiful'

The Gap Band's legendary lead singer Uncle Charlie Wilson serves as a great mentor
to the younger Snoop. Slowly but surely they've explored music making together, this
being their first major breakthrough. Wilson's brilliant shine is saved for the end, while
Pharrell's hit-making falsetto on the hook helped make it one of Snoop's more
successful singles.

Too $hort featuring Jazze Pha: 'Choosin''

One of several singles from $hort's 15th album *Married To The Game*, it is a
marvelous marriage of Jazze's powerhouse soul hooks and $hort in quintessential
player form.

SOUTH/MIDWEST COLLABORATIONS:

Chingy featuring Snoop Dogg and Ludacris: 'Holidae Inn'

The second single from St. Louis rapper Chingy's debut *Jackpot* pairs a woozy, warped
beat with the deft verbal gymnastics of himself and his sharp guests on this pick-up joint.

I-20 featuring Lil Fate, Tity Boi and Chingy: 'Fightin in the Club'

With a tremendous, stomping beat, 20 and friends successfully translate concentrated aggression into a song that's an instant head-nodder.

Kanye West featuring Mr. Bentley: 'Workout Plan (Remix)'
A novelty tune about fat busting from Chicago-based producer/rapper West brings a hilarious musical debut from Farnsworth Bentley, an Atlanta-born executive at P. Diddy's Bad Boy Records who achieved an explosion of media attention while acting as Diddy's high-powered valet and dancing in videos by OutKast among others.

Lil Jon & the East Side Boyz featuring Krayzie Bone featuring Lil Jon: 'I Don't Give A ...'
Krayzie Bone (who came to hip-hop fame as part of Ohio's Bone Thugs N Harmony) has a perfectly swangin' flow to counter Lil Jon & the East Side Boyz' octane-fueled chants.

Ludacris featuring Shawnna: 'What's Your Fantasy?'
Luda's first national hit – a saucy and hilarious cut about getting it on – also introduced Chicago's Shawnna (born Rashawnna Guy, daughter of legendary blues musical Buddy Guy). Also worthy is the remix, which adds Trina and New York's Foxy Brown. (On an actual mixtape, I'd blend 'em both together!)

Murphy Lee featuring Jermaine Dupri: 'Wat Da Hook Gon Be?'
From Nelly's St. Lunatics crew in St. Louis, Murphy Lee justifies the spotlight with this cute tune that builds a clever hook off of questioning what they should use for a hook. Original.

Nelly featuring Lil Wayne: 'For My'
Nelly's debut Country Grammar had a lot of radio-ready fare, but he didn't forget the streets, recruiting New Orleans' Lil Wayne for the assist.

Shawnna featuring Ludacris: 'Shake Dat S**t'
The first single from her debut *Worth Tha Weight* allows the first lady of Disturbing Tha Peace to properly unleash her skills, worthy of any male battle rapper.

Trick Daddy featuring Lil Jon and Twista: 'Let's Go'
Produced by Jim Jonesin in Miami, this thoroughly nails the rock and rap hybrid that many have tried – and few have succeeded – to pull off. Guitar stabs and Ozzy Osbourne vocal textures sampled from Black Sabbath's 'Crazy Train' sound utterly natural in combination with Trick Daddy, Chi-Town rapper Twista and Lil Jon's Godzilla-like chorus.

141

Twista featuring 8Ball, Bishop Don Magic Juan and Too $hort: 'Pimp On'
Calling all pimps, calling all pimps … from chameleon colored alligator shoes and manicures to his'n'hers Lexus automobiles, all of the material bases are covered here in fine fashion.

SOUTH/EAST COAST COLLABORATIONS:

Bone Crusher featuring Busta Rhymes, Cam'ron and Jadakiss: 'Never Scared (Remix)'
What began as a regional record became a song that rappers from all over wanted to get on, and these three East Coast MCs proved themselves more than worthy of the honor, with a tight video to match.

Bravehearts featuring Nas and Lil Jon: 'Quick To Back Down'
I'd be quick to back down too, with Lil Jon snarling the chorus while Nas and the Bravehearts bring the intimidation, New York style. I mean, damn.

David Banner featuring Twista and Busta Rhymes: 'Like a Pimp (Remix)'
Twista once grabbed a spot in the Guinness Book of World Records for the sheer speed of his lyrical delivery, but Busta is one of the few to give him a fair run for his money.

So it's marvellous to hear them square off on David Banner's long-awaited breakthrough club anthem.

Kelis featuring Andre 3000: 'Millionaire'
New York R&B singer Kelis had a huge hit in 2003 with 'Milkshake' off of *Tasty*, but this is the quiet standout of her album.

Produced by Andre 3000, who also guests on the song, it sonically reflects the quirky experimental electronic music of UK artists Squarepusher and Aphex Twin (of whom Andre is a fan).

Jadakiss featuring Anthony Hamilton: 'Why?'
North Carolina soul singer Hamilton lends his achingly beautiful and gritty voice to the chorus of this provocative song which emerged prior to the 2004 Presidential election asking questions such as, 'Why did Bush knock down the towers?'

142

Jay-Z featuring UGK: 'Big Pimpin''

Die-hard UGK fans have mixed feelings (to put it nicely) about this smash hit with New York titan Jay-Z, which brought big mainstream exposure for the duo.

But even if it's a something of a guilty pleasure for purists, the nautical theme of the music (provided by Timbaland) and the verses traded by Pimp C, Bun B and Jay-Z are still infectious.

Nas featuring Ludacris and Doug E. Fresh: 'Virgo'

Old-school New York meets new school Gotham as legendary beatboxer and party igniter Doug E. Fresh steps out in top form while matching wits with Nas. It took a master of ceremonies from Atlanta to glue it all together in an unbreakable way, and the combination is lovely.

Missy Elliott featuring Eve: '4 My People'

Virginia meets Philadelphia as Missy and Eve hit the dancefloor for a gutsy jam inspired by the funky grooves of late '80s Chicago house music.

Mobb Deep featuring Lil Jon: 'Real Gangstaz'

What might seem like an unusual pairing between the New York duo and the 'King of Crunk' has real chemistry.

Lil Jon slows down the beats a bit from his usual pace to match Mobb Deep's East Coast swagger.

OutKast featuring Slick Rick: 'Da Art of Storytelling (Remix)'

Andre 3000 and Big Boi pay homage to old-school UK born and New York bred MC Slick Rick and he tributes right on back via this rare remix.

REPRESENTIN' LOVELY:

Arrested Development: 'Tennessee'

AD's breakout hit was the soul revivalist 'Tennessee,' which is kinda funny, considering they were from Atlanta.

David Banner: 'Mississippi'

His entire career focuses on keeping his home state in the popular consciousness, yet 'Mississippi' is perhaps one of Banner's most heartfelt offerings.

Trick Daddy: nailed the rock and rap hybrid with 'Let's Go.'

8Ball and MJG: 'Memphis City Blues'
As avowed Marvin Gaye fans, I think of this as one of their ways to honor the tradition of 'Inner City Blues.'

Jermaine Dupri featuring Ludacris: 'Welcome To Atlanta'
Two friendly Atlanta tour guides give a brief run-down of what they love about their town. Such is the mercurial nature of nightlife that by the time the remix rolled around, JD had to update the lines in the song which helpfully list which ATL clubs are hot at what times.

Juvenile, Wacko and Skip: 'Nolia Clap'
New Orleans' Magnolia Projects have gotten a lot of exposure through lyrics and videos, but 'Nolia Clap' for once makes it sound more funky than just rough and hard.

Lil Scrappy: 'FILA (Forever I Love Atlanta)'
Lil Jon brings the beats and Lil Scrappy brings the vocal heat in this crunk cut that leaves no doubt as to their allegiance to their home.

Petey Pablo: 'Raise Up'
Putting the Cackalackas on the rap map was no easy feat, but Petey Pablo and producer Timbaland did it permanently with memorable minor key strings and Petey's thunderous chorus: 'North Carolina, c'mon and raise up/Take your shirt off, twist it around your head/Spin it like a helicopter."

Pitbull: 'Welcome To Miami'
After JD's 'Welcome To Atlanta' came this new area-specific version that circulated heavily on the mixtape circuit and lined up the Cuban-American rapper for his debut album M.I.A.M.I. (Money Is a Major Issue).

Scarface featuring Devin and Tela: 'Southside: Houston, Texas'
A raw look at Houston's inner zones, where 'Southern hospitality' rhymes with 'Southern fatality.'

Ying Yang Twins: 'Georgia Dome'
The sequel to 'Get Low,' their massive hit with Lil Jon & the East Side Boyz, clues in the rest of the world to a regionalized term for oral sex.

UNPREDICTABLE COLLABORATIONS:

Baby featuring Toni Braxton: 'Baby You Can Do It'
R&B chanteuse Braxton updates a disco-funk classic by S.O.S. Band on the chorus
while Baby flashes cash on the verses.

Beyoncé featuring Lil Flip: 'Naughty Girl'
They're both from Houston and record for the same label, but Beyoncé (of
Destiny's Child) and Lil Flip were not seemingly destined to appear on a song
together until he was asked to pop on her interpolation of favorites by Donna
Summer and Prince.

Britney Spears featuring Ying Yang Twins: 'I Got That (Boom Boom)'
Like Beyoncé's song, this was not a collaboration in which all artists got in the studio
together to create it. Too bad, for a picture of Britney in full blond pop tart phase in
the booth with D-Roc and Kaine would be worth a thousand words. Instead, this
incongruous song will have to do.

Bubba Sparxxx featuring Justin Timberlake: 'Hootnanny'
Timberlake, who came to fame as part of the boy-band N°Sync, has explored his love
of hip-hop more than other N°Syncers, working with the Neptunes and Timbaland.
He lets loose on this cut with Bubba, showing he's no celebrity elitist.

Cee-Lo featuring John Popper: 'Country Love'
The lead singer of the band Blues Traveler would be off the radar of so many in the
hip-hop community, but here Cee-Lo demonstrates his open-minded musical taste
with a unique duet with John Popper.

Destiny's Child featuring T.I. and Lil Wayne: 'Soldier'
The biggest selling American female group of all time stay in tune with other music
making waves in their time, evidenced in this song that interprets a Southern hip-hop
flow with an R&B twist and presents invited guests who are hot on the street.

Jacki-O featuring Ms. Betty Wright: 'Sleeping With the Enemy'
Ms. Wright is a legend not only of Miami soul, but the international music community
as a songwriter and vocal arranger for countless artists. It's a pleasant surprise to see
her paired in with Jacki-O's freaky tales.

Joe featuring Mystikal: 'Stutter'

A guilty pleasure R&B hit from the East Coast is a mildly accusatory ditty ("I can tell you're lying/Because when you're replying, you stutter …") that turns into something rugged during the 16 bars of verse that New Orleans' Mystikal throws down.

Santana featuring Lauryn Hill and Cee-Lo: 'Do You Like the Way'

Carlos Santana's mega album *Supernatural* has the legendary guitarist collaborating with a host of hot young talent. From the urban music world, the wise one came calling on New York's Lauryn Hill to weave magic with Cee-Lo in a startling duet.

Teena Marie featuring Baby: 'I'm Still In Love'

Even stranger than Baby with Toni Braxton is Teena Marie with Baby, who created the Cash Money Classics label in order to put out Teena's *La Dona* in 2004.

CONTROVERSIAL JAMS:

2 Live Crew: 'The F—k Shop'

Part of the *As Nasty As They Wanna Be* album which ignited a fight for free speech in the Supreme Court, 'The F—k Shop' was responsible for another lawsuit: For sampling guitar licks from Van Halen's 'Ain't Talkin' 'Bout Love.'

Goodie Mob: 'One Monkey Don't Stop No Show'

The "monkey" in question refers to several situations including losing their long-time record deal and a car accident that took Khujo Goodie's leg. But it was more-than-subtly suggested by the band, and overtly proclaimed by the hip-hop media at the time of release, that the title of both this song and their 2004 album had more to do with the departure of Cee-Lo from the group.

Jacki-O: 'P***y (Real Good)'

Her debut single sent Miami Beach clubs into orgiastic frenzy, got her banned from MTV and BET and catalyzed a host of creepy stalkers. All because of a little kitty.

Lil Flip: 'Game Over'

People have to admit how clever the music on Flip's song is – everyone except video game company Namco, that is. They sued for copyright infringement after hearing sounds from their classic arcade games Pac-Man and Ms. Pac-Man lifted to form the track's instrumental.

Ludacris: 'Blow It Out'

He keeps it civilized, but you'll hear a slight dig at Bill O'Reilly as well as other critics, while eerie *Psycho*-like minor key stabs in the background emphasize the point.

OutKast: 'Bombs Over Baghdad'

Released a year before 9/11, this stopped being something one heard on the radio after the Towers fell, falling on a list of sensitive songs to be placed to the side. As a groundbreaking record shattering more boundaries between hip-hop and fast-paced electronic dance music, it's truly a shame.

OutKast: 'Rosa Parks'

What clearly began as a joyous song celebrating black American heritage turned into a 5-plus year drama as the caregiver and lawyer for the elderly and ill civil rights activist sued on her behalf for using her name (which only appears in the title and not the actual lyrics).

T.I.: '99 Problems (Lil Flip Ain't One)'

The battle between Lil Flip and T.I. extended across interviews, public appearances and songs for mixtapes, including this most incisive take over the instrumental for Jay-Z's '99 Problems.'

Ying Yang Twins: 'Whistle (While You Twurk)'

If they were truly free, Snow White and the Seven Dwarfs themselves would probably get crunk and take their clothes off to this stripper anthem that brought the Twins to national attention, but their owners did not appreciate it and expressed it in lawsuit form.

Young Buck featuring T.I. and Ludacris: 'Stomp'

A unique track that was a popular mixtape hit, 'Stomp' features two guests that are actually verbally sniping at each other on the same song! The final version on Buck's album substitutes Los Angeles rapper Game for T.I.'s verse, but Luda's still stands.

JUST SAY NO:

Big Moe: 'Purple Stuff'

Houston's Big Moe has two albums that address his town's proclivities towards sipping syrup (Purple Stuff and City of Syrup), but this gangstafied R&B cut is the best.

Veterans of 10 years in the hip-hop business, Goodie Mob shared the limelight with a chimp to promote their 2004 album, One Monkey Don't Stop No Show.

Body Head Bangers Featuring YoungBloodZ: 'I Smoke, I Drank'
It's always fun when people celebrate their inability to shake their party addictions, as these guys do so well here.

Gangsta Pat: 'Smoke Somethin'
Marijuana anthems have disproportionately come from the West Coast, but Pat puts it down for the stoners in Memphis.

I-20 featuring Three 6 Mafia: 'Hennessy and Hydro'
20 invites some of his favorite artists to kick back and party with him, capturing a divine form of disorientation within the groove.

Ludacris featuring Lil Flip: 'Screwed Up'
Luda and Flip assume the roles of the Dirty South's Cheech and Chong while paying lyrical and sonic tribute to the late DJ Screw.

Master P: 'Mr. Ice Cream Man'
The origins of this song are controversial (Bay Area MC Yukmouth says he first came up with the concept), but 'Mr. Ice Cream Man' finds Master P at the height of his crack dealing exploits on wax.

Three 6 Mafia: 'Sippin' (On Some Syrup)'
By the time this song about leaning back hit the streets, curiosity from the international hip-hop community for the specialty drink of the South was more than piqued.

Three 6 Mafia: 'Rainbow Colors'
Once you've sipped enough syrup and inhaled enough intoxicants, the colors are bound to be nothing but lively, as Three 6 captures so well in sound.

T.I.: 'Dope Boyz'
Dedicated to the drug dealers on the grind getting money, 'Dope Boyz' details some intricacies of the crack trade.

YoungBloodZ: 'Taquila'
Atlanta duo Sean Paul and J-Bo make the fiery liquid their girl and the object of a very drunken love song.

ALBUM RECOMMENDATIONS

A lot of the artists mentioned here have helped the Dirty South attract and build an audience outside its home. Others have achieved classic status in the region while escaping international notice and leaving everyone else none the wiser – until now.

This is not meant to be a list of every essential purchase. Some albums deemed completely necessary by music critics and superfans may not be here at all; but then those folks may have missed some of these gems. Ahh, subjectivity! The point is that there are a great many titles to choose from, and one could do far worse than to start – or enhance – a Dirty South collection with these albums.

Arrested Development

It's kind of shocking how history seems to be diminishing the contributions of Arrested Development, nearly writing the group out of the picture. With over four million copies sold, their debut album *3 Years, 5 Months And 2 Days In The Life Of …* (Chrysalis/EMI, 1992) painted a soulful and earthy portrait of the South to the mainstream music world. Covering Sly Stone's 'People Everyday,' the comparisons were almost inevitable, but Arrested Development was a spicy stew that also absorbed elements of Southern blues and the East Coast 'Daisy Age' hip-hop popularized by groups like De La Soul and A Tribe Called Quest.

Baby

After years of appearing on other people's albums and as part of the Big Tymers on Cash Money Records, Baby finally stepped out on his own on *Birdman* (Cash Money, 2002). In-house producer Mannie Fresh handles studio duties for a large percentage of Cash Money tracks, so he's present, of course. But *Birdman* is one of the most varied Cash Money releases thanks to contributions from Jazze Pha ('Do That,' featuring P. Diddy), the Neptunes ('What Happened To That Boy?') and Timbaland ('Baby You Can Do It,' with Toni Braxton).

David Banner: Mississippi's champion broke through in 2003 after years in the underground.

B.G.

Chopper City In The Ghetto (Cash Money, 1999) is a key release in the history of Cash Money and its journey from the Magnolia Projects in New Orleans to wide recognition. Incredibly, it was B.G.'s fifth album, having recorded his first record locally when he was 11 years old. Simmering street hit 'Cash Money Is An Army,' and ode to status 'Bling Bling,' imprinted B.G.'s distinctive voice (kind of a deep rasp) on the mainstream rap world. Meanwhile, *Life After Cash Money* (Chopper City/KOCH, 2004) allows a glimpse into B.G.'s evolution as a man and the proprietor of his own label.

David Banner

Mississippi: The Album (SRC/Universal, 2003) is a statement of purpose for Banner, providing a snapshot of life in the country's most overlooked state and giving it a point of pride.

After lingering for years in the underground, his superhero-like energy and deep, dark voice got the whole South crunk with banging club hits such as 'Like a Pimp,' which he also produced, and he's been able to maintain that sort of level. Hot on its heels, *MTA2: Baptized In Dirty Water* (SRC/Universal, 2004) picks up where its predecessor left off and moves right in closer to grab listeners and reveal a bit more of his grit and struggle.

Big Gipp

Renowned for his work as part of the Goodie Mob, Gipp chose an intergalactic funk flavor for his solo album *Mutant Mindframe* (In The Paint/Goodie Mob Records/KOCH, 2003).

This is personified best by his collaboration with Andre 3000, 'Boogie Man,' a weightless electronic romp into an outernational sound. The easy swing of 'Steppin Out' with Sleepy Brown made for an ideal radio/rollerskating jam, while 8Ball guests on another standout, the sex-you-down joint 'All Over Your Body' and Goodie Mob partners T-Mo and Khujo jump in for the token aggressive cut, 'Let's Fight.'

Bone Crusher

High off the success of the breakthrough hit 'Never Scared' in clubs, sporting events and on the radio, *AttenCHUN!* (So So Def, 2003) woke up the public to a 350-pound sensation with a voice and heart to match the big frame.

His talent for writing solid hooks is clear here, and his skills have since been in demand from other artists. He took the time to make sure the oft-delayed follow-up *Fight Music* (So So Def/BMG, 2005) advanced Bone's personal story and topped the energy reached on *AttenCHUN!*

Cee-Lo

No sense in hiding that Cee-Lo is one of my favorites, an extraordinary artist who, despite much critical praise, is still quite underrated for being both a dextrous rapper and a soul-stirring singer, not to mention a budding producer in his own right. (That's what we call a triple threat.)

His eclectic debut solo album *Cee-Lo Green And His Perfect Imperfections* (Arista, 2002) broke him through to the non-hip-hop listening audience with the horn-y funk fest 'Closet Freak' and revealed layers of versatility he wasn't able to express in the Goodie Mob. Sophomore album *Cee-Lo Green Is … The Soul Machine* (Arista, 2004) has brought me much happiness in its first year of release, flirting with gospel house, classic soul, blues and quick'n'quirky rap. It still sounds fresh to my ears every time I hear it – which, I assure you, rarely happens with the hundreds of albums I listen to (and never revisit) as I go about my business of writing.

Devin The Dude

Tilted just a little bit to the left of nearly everything else is the always-refreshing Devin The Dude. It's hard to go wrong with the man who always puts much-needed comic relief or a relaxed vibe into anything he appears on, from his own songs to his numerous guest spots. *To Tha X-Treme* (Rap-A-Lot, 2004) begins with a megamix of various songs called 'Devin's Medley' which sets the tone nicely. 'Anythang' is a sublimely chilled balance to funnily flirty tracks such as 'Come On & Come.'

DJ Magic Mike

Orlando's bass pioneer/scratch wizard has a staggering amount of CDs available spanning more than 15 years of gleefully wrecking car stereo systems. *Foundations of Bass Vol. 1* (Cheetah Records, 1997) does a nice job of compiling a variety of earlier work along with songs that were new to that release. But, then again, the newer *Greatest Hits* (Cheetah Records, 2004) is oh-so convenient.

Dungeon Family

The only album for the Dungeon Family (a collective which includes Organized Noize, OutKast and Goodie Mob), *Even In Darkness* (Arista, 2001) is remembered in somewhat melancholy terms. A solid album just overflowing with ridiculous amounts of talent at every turn, it was overshadowed by other projects and not given the solid push that it needed to really get it out there. A video was made for the Kraftwerk-inspired 'Trans D.F. Express' with OutKast, Cee-Lo, Big Gipp and Backbone, but the song is only one of several highlights. OutKast's former production alias ET3 splits production duties with Organized Noize. Heck, if it were to be re-released it could spawn some new smash singles.

Big Gipp: a member of the Goodie Mob, Gipp chose an intergalactic funk theme for his 2003 solo album.

8Ball (right) and MJG: Expertly blending gospel and the street.

8Ball and MJG

Named after a Marvin Gaye album title, *In Our Lifetime* (Draper, Inc., 1999) was released several years into their career and finds them at a point of self-evaluation. As such, it makes a great introduction for those who didn't follow their earlier albums. On it, they share lessons in the music business learned the hard way on 'Paid Dues' (featuring Cee-Lo), one of several songs that show them dropping knowledge.

Space Age 4 Eva (JCOR, 2001) is often cited as an album that people love for the futuristic pimp flow. Meanwhile, *Living Legends* (Bad Boy, 2004) and lead single (the crunked-up 'You Don't Want Drama') brought them back into the forefront with a strong album that availed itself of both their own and P. Diddy's Bad Boy resources. Standout track 'Straight Cadillac Pimpin'"(featuring male vocalist Shannon Jones) expertly blends the gospel with the street with its lyrics and the hums of a choir driving the music.

Geto Boys

Besides flaunting that infamous cover, *We Can't Be Stopped* (Rap-A-Lot, 1995) has the Geto Boys' most recognizable anthem, the paranoid/schizophrenic exposé 'Mind Playing Tricks On Me' and straight up raw reality tracks like 'Another Nigger In The Morgue' and 'Fuck A War.'

Of course, it is also easy/lazy to fast-forward and check some of the highlights of their career on their *Greatest Hits* (Rap-A-Lot, 2002). At the time of this writing they were also readying the release of a reunion album.

Goodie Mob

People interested in the Dirty South should be ordered to purchase a few releases, and *Soul Food* (LaFace, 1995) certainly fits into that category with its strong social message and literal music for starved souls.

Here I go again recommending a 'best of' type release, but *Dirty South Classics* (LaFace, 2003) was compiled to be a one-stop Goodie shop. Of course that doesn't include any material from the newer, three-man incarnation of the group –that's all been reserved for the controversial *One Monkey Don't Stop No Show* (Goodie Mob Records/KOCH, 2004).

Mannie Fresh

The man responsible for something like 90 per cent of the work on Cash Money took a relatively long time to drop his own solo album, but when he finally did it was *Real Big* (Cash Money, 2004). Fresh is one of the strongest of the vanguard of Southern producers to place real instruments and players above the art of sampling, and it shows on this effort.

I-20

Self-Explanatory (Capitol, 2004) is a well-rounded debut album that introduces an MC who can present solid advice for lost young girls ('Kisha') just as soon as hop on a bounce track with Juvenile ('Point Them Out'), get screwed with Three 6 Mafia on 'Hennessy and Hydro' or engage in some aural sex ('Slow Fucking' featuring Shawnna). Versatility rules the new South, and it will only get better for 20 as he reveals more layers over time.

Jacki-O

It kicks off with the coochie pride of 'P°°°y (Real Good),' but sex doesn't lead Jacki's debut *Poe Little Rich Girl* (TVT, 2004) as much as one would think. Her hustle in life is strong and she translates her business and street sense into entertaining stories. It's clear that, although she's fierce, she doesn't take herself too seriously, which makes her an artist it's easy to relate to.

Juvenile

400 Degreez (Cash Money, 1998) is a seminal release that helped put Cash Money on the national radar in a big way. First single 'Ha' trained non-Southern ears to a new porch flow – in this case, one that literally placed the word 'ha' at the end of every sentence. By the time the second single 'Back That Azz Up' hit MTV and BET, middle aged secretaries and pre-teens alike were doing just as guest Lil Wayne instructed: "After you back it up and stop/Now drop it like it's hot." *Juve The Great* (Cash Money, 2004) was a runaway success on the Billboard charts thanks to 'Slow Motion' (with the late Soulja Slim) and its poise on the precipice of a new era without Cash Money is impressive.

Killer Mike

Here's yet another underrated talent, this time from the Dungeon Family. *Monster* (Sony, 2003) generated the, well, monster jam 'Akshon (Yeah!),' which dovetailed nicely with the national recognition earned from his appearance on OutKast's 'The Whole World,' yet the album wasn't given the overall attention it merited. He took it back to the streets, releasing the appropriately titled *Dat Crack* with Grind Time Official (Grindhouse, 2003), a rare chance to hear unfettered thoughts almost in reaction to the major label situation. He was in the lab for a while working on his album for 2005, which will likely have even more to lend itself to listeners than these do.

Lil Jon & the East Side Boyz

Kings of Crunk (TVT, 2002) spawned 'Get Low,' the insatiable hit that was still almost as likely to get airplay two years after its release. *Part II* (TVT, 2003) expands on the biggest hit of *Kings of Crunk* with new remixes of 'Get Low' and adds a bonus DVD with videos and great behind-the-scenes footage including a rare glimpse of Lil Jon at work in the studio. But *Crunk Juice* (TVT, 2004) is truly their pièce de resistance to date, with a staggering amount of talented guests including Ice Cube ('Roll Call'), Usher and Ludacris ('Lovers & Friends') and comedian Chris Rock in several interludes. In many ways, it's the album that justifies their mainstream recognition.

Lil Wayne

Wayne took a cheeky jab at Juvenile's *400 Degreez* album when he named his *500 Degreez* (Cash Money, 2002) as a way to suggest extra hotness. But previous offering *Tha Block Is Hot* (Cash Money, 1999), with its tension building title track, is actually a more sizzling album to find. *Tha Carter* (Cash Money, 2004) may end up being best remembered for its first single 'Go DJ,' and the video in which Wayne escapes from Hannibal Lecter-style shackles in a prison to rock the mic. But Wayne and longtime producer Mannie Fresh show the effortless interplay that friends and family share on other potential hits like the mission statement implicit in 'Cash Money Millionaires.'

Ludacris

As he's another personal favorite, I have trouble picking the best Ludacris recommendation. It's really hard to go wrong with any of his albums and they're all worth owning. *Chicken N Beer* (Def Jam South, 2003) especially pops out for its numerous, varied hits (the adult 'P-Poppin,' childhood reminiscence 'Diamond in the Back,' the sexy and sassy 'Splash Waterfalls,' the Kanye West-produced 'Stand Up'). *Red Light District* (Def Jam South, 2004) is multifaceted and surprising in that it would appear on the surface to be about zones of sexual liberty –it is, on certain songs. But it is a larger metaphor for his freedom of speech as his album represents that free space where he can do or say whatever he wants.

OutKast

Again with the favorites and the dilemmas! This time I'm going to be even a bit more wishy-washy about it and just attempt to order dear readers to explore each of OutKast's albums, from the honest, unfettered pimp style of *Southernplayalisticadillacmuzik* (La Face, 1994) and the rather more experimental albums *ATLiens* (La Face, 1996) and *Aquemini* (La Face, 1998) to the album which catapulted them deep into the center of the mainstream, *Stankonia* (La Face, 2000). *Big Boi And Dre Present … OutKast* (La Face, 2001) is a 'greatest hits so far' type of collection for those who might want to (shamefully) skip the first four albums in favor of a Cliff's Notes version. The double album *Speakerboxx/The Love Below* (La Face, 2003) is somewhat of a masterpiece that allows each member to stretch out in their

161

own personal field of vision. Big Boi stays booming with bass on the streets while Andre 3000 imagines himself the lead in a European romance musical. So distinctly different from each other yet so complimentary, OutKast only get stronger with age.

Petey Pablo

North Carolina's Pablo is blessed with a voice and tone that doesn't sound like anyone else. His sly yet assertive delivery has won him the accolades and efforts of top producers. Timbaland gave Pablo's debut album *Diary Of A Sinner: 1st Entry* (Jive, 2001) the hit 'Raise Up,' and Lil Jon provided the beat for the hoochie inspired radio and video smash 'Freak-A-Leak' for the sophomore album *Still Writing In My Diary* (Jive, 2004). His next chapter, which appears to be affiliated with notorious West Coast label Death Row (now called Tha Row), is already being written.

Pastor Troy

His father is the real Pastor Troy, as in a pastor of the church, but Troy's incendiary style reads of a real God-given talent to communicate with people. To get an idea of the fire deep in the belly of Atlanta's hip-hop scene, listen to the focus that he holds across his albums, particularly the anthemic *We Ready: I Declare War* (Madd Society, 1999) and *By Any Means Necessary* (Universal, 2004).

Scarface

Those looking to study will dig back in the vaults for *The World Is Yours* (Priority, 1993), but those with tough purchase choices to make that are looking for the bottom line can be very happy with the *Greatest Hits* (Rap-A-Lot, 2002). It even includes 'Guess Who's Back?' (featuring Jay-Z and Beanie Sigel) from the album which came out the same year – *The Fix* (Def Jam South, 2002), which also spawned the hit 'On My Block' with its accompanying video shot in Houston's Fifth Ward.

Soulja Slim

The tragedy of Soulja Slim being killed in 2003 in front of his mother's house will not be soon diminished. A star and trendsetter in the making, who was extraordinarily popular in his home of New Orleans, he was snuffed out in his prime. The irony that it happened as his collaboration with Juvenile ('Slow Motion') was entering the Billboard charts is not lost. *Years Later ... A Few Months After* (KOCH, 2003), his last album, has another song with Juvenile as well as several other charismatic offerings ('Lov Me Lov Me Not,' 'Souljas On My Feet,' 'Yeahh').

2 Live Crew

Of course, no Southern collection is going to be complete without the legendary *As*

The late Soulja Slim, gunned down in 2003 on his mother's front lawn.

Nasty As They Wanna Be (Luke Records, 1989), a landmark in free speech and an entertaining lowbrow listen besides, inspired in part by the no-holds-barred outrageousness of comedians like Richard Pryor and Blowfly.

For me it was a perfect record to sneak in the house at age 16 to hear what all the fuss on the news was about and just how different the clean and dirty versions of songs like 'Me So Horny' could be. There were subsequent 2 Live Crew releases (the group even continued on after Luke's departure in the 1990s), but none captured the simple glory and incendiary sass of *Nasty*.

T.I.

Trap Muzik (Grand Hustle/Atlantic, 2003) shone light on a charismatic new star in Atlanta as well as the severity of the dope game where he used to grind. The David Banner-produced 'Rubberband Man' earned him a first mainstream hit and appeared to telescope an upward rise in his career.

After spending a large part of 2004 sidelined behind bars for a parole violation, T.I. came out with even more talent and vigor at the end of the year with *Urban Legend* (Grand Hustle/Atlantic, 2004). It features the appropriately titled 'Bring 'Em Out,' a bombastic single produced by the East Coast's in-demand Swizz Beats and featuirng Jay-Z on the hook, and an array of guests and producers like Lil Kim, B.G., Trick Daddy, Lil Wayne, Mannie Fresh, Jazze Pha and the Neptunes.

Though the music is more widely accessible, T.I. has managed to keep his motivations intact.

Timbaland

Timbaland has produced so many incredible songs for other artists, but it's difficult to find one concentrated CD collection that showcases his adaptability to effectively work with different musicians.

He's recorded several albums with rapper Magoo, but the full-length to find is his proper solo album, *Tim's Bio: Life From Da Bassment* (Blackground/Virgin, 1998), a truly under-appreciated effort. From 'Fat Rabbit,' which introduced the instantly memorable young Ludacris to late singer Aaliyah's harmonious sizzler 'John Blaze,' Timbaland tackles hip-hop and R&B with equal panache and innovation – he's literally changed the game in both genres.

Too $hort

In 2005, Too $hort will release his 16th album – a landmark in any music career but particularly within hip-hop. His 15th, *Married To The Game* (Jive), is easily one of his best – though not an instant platinum hit like most of his others. I find that curious, between the crunk chorus of 'Shake That Monkey' (featuring Lil Jon), the infectious

R&B funk of 'How It Goes Down' (featuring Oobie) and 'Choosin' (featuring Jazze Pha) and the traditional West Coast bump of 'Burn Rubber.' Here more than anywhere else, $hort melds his seamless mack flow with a high level of musicality. Album number 16 will be mainly produced by Lil Jon and Jazze Pha.

Trick Daddy

The man whose full rap alias is Trick Daddy Dollars ('T Double D' for short) has six albums under his belt, each with something to offer listeners.

His most recent efforts, though, show a man increasingly at ease with an ability to craft street anthems as well as popular hits. *Thug Holiday* (Slip-N-Slide/Atlantic, 2002) emerged with the insanely catchy 'In Da Wind' (featuring Cee-Lo), the spiritual 'God's Been Good' (featuring Betty Wright's Children's Choir) and the hardened 'Gangsta' and 'Money & Drugs.'

Meanwhile, *Thug Matrimony: Married To The Streets* (Slip-N-Slide/Atlantic, 2004) bounded out the gate on the strength of the Ozzy Osbourne-sampling 'Let's Go' (featuring Lil Jon and Twista). It provides many counterpoints to that headbanger, including another sweet pop tune, 'Sugar (Gimme Some)' (featuring Cee-Lo and Ludacris) where one may hear Trick actually singing on the chorus, his deep tones harmonizing with Cee-Lo's elevated range. Others would be scared to be on such a gentle song, but Trick still comes out with his necessary edge.

UGK

UGK (Underground Kingz) didn't realize when they came up with their name that it would be somewhat of a self-fulfilling prophecy, as Bun B himself relates in the *Dirty States of America* documentary.

I'm one of those UGK fans that came to the group relatively late into their career. So some might find this sacrilegious, but there really isn't a better value for newcomers than to get the *Best of UGK* (Jive, 2003). The collection spans the highlights of the first phase of their career, until Pimp C (one-half of the group) was sent to jail in 2002 for violating parole on an aggravated assault conviction, a charge he and his lawyer contest and are working to overturn. It provides a solid aural blueprint of what so many have followed both in confident swagger and sound, from rappers all over the South to East Coast titans like Jay-Z, who was definitely listening from afar. To dig a little bit deeper, look for *Ridin' Dirty* (Jive, 1996) and the guest-spot collection *Side Hustles Featuring UGK* (Jive, 2002). Most recently there is the independently released *Live From The Harris County Jail* (Pimp C Family Records, 2004), a brazen solo project from the incarcerated Pimp C under the alias Sweet James Jones. The UGK mystique has snowballed in recent years, making the next phase of their career that much more exciting to anticipate.

Ying Yang Twins

Me & My Brother (TVT, 2003) made the Ying Yang Twins a hip-hop household name with 'Salt Shaker' (featuring Lil Jon & the East Side Boyz) and sports anthem 'What's Happnin!' with Trick Daddy. More recently, they've released *My Brother & Me* (TVT, 2004). It's a collection of various Twins appearances on remixes of other people's songs (such as Juvenile's 'Slow Motion') as well as a few new remixes of 'Salt Shaker.'

There's also a bonus DVD of live performances as well as videos for 'Salt Shaker,' 'Naggin'' and 'What's Happnin!' Intended to tide people over until their next full-length release, it is actually a smarter purchase if choosing only one since the visual performance aspect of the group (as captured on the DVD) greatly enriches the picture of the Twins.

YoungBloodZ

Recorded when they were relative young'uns, *Against Da Grain* (La Face, 1999) made a huge impact throughout the South but especially in their native Atlanta with crunk club hits 'Shakem' Off' and 'U-Way.' Who wouldn't appreciate a good drinking record, even if your proclivity is not towards tipples? *Drankin Patnaz* (La Face, 2003) is just such a delight, as much a dedication to J-Bo and Sean Paul's beloved pastime as a textbook into the crunk lifestyle. Lil Jon joins them on the production and chorus of 'Damn!' – their one-way ticket into the national hip-hop arena. Bottoms up!

COMPILATIONS:

This section concludes with some brief picks for various artists collections, also called compilations. These are traditionally good value for consumers looking to take a chance on hearing music and artists that are previously unfamiliar, or to find rare material.

Bass Mixx Party-Club Classics (Little Joe, 1999)

Largely comprised of 2 Live Crew/Luke party jams ('Hoochie Mama,' 'It's Your Birthday'), including a 2 Live megamix, there are also Miami bass vets like Lejuan Love.

Crunk and Disorderly (TVT, 2003)

What ostensibly began as a crunk Christmas album instead came out as part holiday and part everyday when they didn't have enough songs; still, the seasonal jams (David

Banner's 'It's Christmas Time (Jingle Bells),' Killer Mike's 'A Christmas Grind,' Ying Yang Twins' 'Ho! Ho!') are what make this compilation distinctive.

Crunk Classics (TVT, 2004)

TVT could have stacked this compilation with only TVT material (a common device for record labels), but instead they curated a more true reflection of the crunk scene with huge anthems like YoungBloodZ' 'U-Way,' Rasheeda's 'Do It' (featuring Pastor Troy and Re Re) and Archie Eversole's 'We Ready.'

The Day After Hell Broke Loose (Rap-A-Lot, 2004)

Houston's Rap-A-Lot has consistently brought out good music for a very long time, as evidenced by this collection which brings highlights from Devin The Dude, Chamillionaire, Slim Thug, Lil Flip and Mike Jones.

Dirty South Booty Freaknik (Little Joe, 2001)

Convenient access to predictable cuts from Miami bass staples Poison Clan, Uncle Al (whose songs make up most of the track listing) and, of course, Luke.

Down South Bounce Vols. 1-3 (2001-2003, Warlock)

DJ Jelly, a popular jock from Atlanta's Big Oomp Records (an empire in itself with several record store outlets), helms these well-done compilations that are all to be recommended. Balanced among the different hotspots of the South, many styles are represented but all are hits in one way or another.

Down South Hustlers: Bouncin' and Swingin' The Value Pack Compilation (Priority, 1995)

A rare double-disc set predating No Limit Records' deal with Priority, with songs from Mia X, 8Ball and MJG, E.S.G., Magnolia Slim (later Soulja Slim) and Master P.

Get Crunk! (Tommy Boy, 1999)

Crunk as both a term and a movement didn't really hit the popular consciousness until around 2003 at best, but not for lack of a recognizable record label like Tommy Boy trying to make it happen much earlier with this solid collection. There's early work from David Banner's Crooked Lettaz as well as highlights from Three 6 Mafia, Lil Jon & the East Side Boyz, Mystikal, UGK and 8Ball and MJG.

I'm Bout It (No Limit, 1997)

The soundtrack to the straight-to-video classic from Master P brings hardcore contributions from UGK, E-40, 8Ball and MJG and others.

Mean Green: Major Players Compilation (No Limit/Priority, 1998)

A classic South meets West offering, where the Left Coast's Too $hort, Mack 10, E-40 and B-Legit share billing with Mystikal, C-Murder and, of course, Master P.

Real Recognize Real (Trill City Records, 2004)

Two of Houston's foundational hip-hop DJs (O.G. Ron C and Bro. Wood) offer a double-disc set of the finest from their town and beyond. Disc two is "chopped and screwed."

Rhythm & Quad 166 Vol. 1 (Elektra, 1998)

This celebration of the Atlanta bass sound as it veered into R&B territory yielded the radio hit 'Swing My Way' by KP & Envyi. It also reveals the roots of crunk, featuring some early productions by Lil Jon. It's called Vol. 1, but there were no subsequent editions.

Six O'Clock Vol. 1 (Slip-N-Slide/Atlantic, 2001)

Atlanta radio DJ Greg Street curated this selection which includes songs from OutKast, Trick Daddy, UGK, Jazze Pha and Ludacris, plus freestyles from EPMD's Erick Sermon and 8Ball.

So So Def Bass Allstars Vol. 3 (So So Def, 1998)

When Lil Jon was as an A&R for Jermaine Dupri's label, these collections were the centerpiece of his work. I'm partial to Vol. 3, which features Inoj's popular cover of Cyndi Lauper's 'Time After Time' and New Edition's Ricky Bell on 'When Will I See You Smile Again?'

The South Will Rise Again ... This Time It Won't Be The Same (South Will Rise, 2000)

Besides being frighteningly correct in its prediction, this compilation is a fairly eclectic assemblage of tunes from the likes of Big Boi, Kingpin Skinny Pimp and Goodie Mob alongside lesser known names like DJ Jubilee and Playa Fly.

MEDIA CENTER

Resources for further Dirty South grazing

PUBLICATIONS

Inspired by the success of the South's independent record labels, an independent magazine industry is beginning to blossom there as well. Many of these publications are free, have a circulation of 50,000 copies or fewer, and do not have national or international distribution. Usually, the best way for those outside their immediate reach to check out these titles is to subscribe. That is also a helpful way to support these growing businesses, often started and staffed by undying fans of the music.

In recent years, New York-based national magazines *The Source*, *XXL* and *Vibe* have started to include consistent coverage of Southern artists and cities, and are usually worth perusing for those feature stories. But it is encouraging to see the launch of publications outside the traditional American media centers documenting the culture around them. Launching a publication is no easy feat and the odds for survival are daunting. As someone who has worked at and for independent magazines for my entire career, I salute these titles for daring to be successful.

Top Pick:
Ozone Magazine
http://www.ozonemag.com
Publisher/editor Julia Beverly, who has contributed a number of photographs to this book, works tirelessly to produce a strong magazine to represent Southern hip-hop. Based in Orlando, Florida, Beverly and her contributors comb the region to talk to new talent as well as the most popular artists, often capturing the edgier or more honest sides that they might carefully tuck away in other interviews. *Ozone* is also a

refreshing rarity in the magazine industry for making full issues available free to read online.

A.C.E. Entertainment Magazine
http://www.acemagonline.com
This slim, pocket-sized 'zine comes from the West Palm Beach area of Florida and mixes profiles of unsigned and up-and-coming artists with club and event photos.

Atlanta Fever
http://www.atlantafever.com
Covering the music and celebrity scene of the ATL, *Atlanta Fever* talks to the local artists and movers and shakers that make it a hot city.

Block 2 Block Magazine
http://www.block2blockonline.com
Based in Grand Prairie, Texas, *Block 2 Block* focuses on the music emerging from the streets of Texas, Louisiana, Oklahoma and Arkansas (where the magazine is distributed).

Creative Loafing
http://www.creativeloafing.com
An independent mini-chain of free weekly alternative newspapers in Georgia (Atlanta), North Carolina (Charlotte) and Florida (Tampa). For locals and visitors, the *Creative Loafing* titles (archived online) are normally a good source for club and concert listings as well as music features (which are occasionally about hip-hop).

Crunk Magazine
http://www.crunkmag.com
It's billed as a "fashion, music and entertainment magazine," but *Crunk's* focus is still on the music and popular artists of the Dirty South. It also has a free weekly email newsletter (sign up online).

Don Diva Magazine
http://www.dondivamag.com
Don Diva hails from New York and only occasionally features interviews with Dirty South artists. But it's somewhat unique in the hip-hop world, a lifestyle mag that caters to ballers with its look at high-end fashion, jewelry, security and technology alongside the music. In that respect it addresses a Southern desire to shine.

Fish 'n' Grits Magazine
http://www.fishngrits.com
A magazine smart enough to take advantage of the crossover between hip-hop and the

world of adult entertainment, the unfortunately titled *Fish 'n' Grits* finds rappers occasionally posing for pictorials with porn stars and strippers. There's stuff to read, too, but I'm not sure how many people actually get to that part.

Gangsta Rap Coloring Book by Aye Jay (Last Gasp)
http://www.ayejay.com
In the miscellaneous department, this is not a magazine, but an actual coloring book, like it says. Southern California artist Aye Jay offers black and white drawings of rappers for coloring. The South figures strongly in the book, with renditions of people like Scarface, Master P, Trick Daddy, and even (curious choice) DJ Screw. Some are better than others but all are amusing – especially if you draw flowers coming out of people's guns.

Tha Hole
http://www.thahole.com
Straight outta Huntsville, Alabama, *Tha Hole* covers artists from throughout the South, with past cover stars including David Banner, Choppa and Camouflage.

Houston Press
http://www.houstonpress.com
Part of the national *New Times* chain of free alternative weekly newspapers (to which, full disclosure, I am a contributor), *Houston Press* features concert and club previews and event listings. The *New Times* chain also archives full issues online.

Memphis Flyer
http://www.memphisflyer.com
Another alternative newsweekly, this one from Memphis, Tennessee, covering local beats and events as well as news and culture in the community.

Miami New Times
http://www.miaminewtimes.com
This newspaper (another *New Times* title) covers the local hip-hop scene, which includes a growing number of national artists and producers who record in the area. Also a good source for club listings, concert picks and reviews.

Murder Dog Magazine
http://www.murderdog.com
Based in Vallejo, California, *Murder Dog* has been one of the most significant supporters of the Dirty South, particularly at a time when other national hip-hop magazines wouldn't lend much ink. Proof positive of the love exchange between the South and the Bay Area, *Murder Dog* continues to profile artists at the heart of the streets.

The New Power
http://www.newpowermagazine.com

Quarterly publication *The New Power* (from Columbus, Mississippi) prides itself on profiling artists and labels that other magazines might deem too new or small, while also keeping an ear to the larger players. Look for informative articles demystifying the process of getting into the music business.

Scratch Magazine
http://www.scratchmagazine.com

Launched in 2004 by Harris Publications (who also publish *XXL* and mens' mag *King*), *Scratch* is a top-notch title covering hip-hop DJs and producers in technical depth. In its first year, Scratch brought out some of the most insightful interviews with Lil Jon, Jazze Pha and Mannie Fresh yet seen in any magazine, enlightening readers as to the secret weapons of their favorite superproducers.

Street Masters Magazine
Phone: 901.888.1003

The first hip-hop magazine to come out of Memphis, *Street Masters* began in 2003 and continues to reach out to the rest of the South with a regional (and not just local) focus.

Streetz Magazine
http://www.streetzmag.com

Streetz concentrates on the flavors emerging from the Southeast, and its main audience is based in Virginia (Richmond, Hampton Roads), Maryland (Baltimore) and Washington DC.

Strip Joint Magazine
http://www.stripjointmag.com

Despite its title, *Strip Joint* actually explores the intersection of music and stripping (see the 'Anatomy of a Hit' chapter in this book) by profiling artists and record labels as well as dancers and 'gentlemen's clubs.'

Urban Pages Magazine
Phone: 843.747.5131

Urban Pages comes from Charleston, South Carolina and focuses on the music and scene bubbling from the streets close to home.

FILMS

This list of recommendations is a bit of a mixed bag, from documentaries and comedies to musicals – and even a porno. The Dirty South is only just beginning to tap the potential of film; expect an explosion of movies of all types to be made in the next several years.

Hollywood would do well to explore the endlessly fascinating life stories to be found in the Southern hip-hop community. (My suggestion: Start with Uncle Luke!) Considering that one could say the same about many icons of hip-hop on the East Coast, whose stories are just begging to be told in cinematic form and still haven't been optioned, it's going to take the Tinseltown dream machine a long time to drive its squeaky wheels onto Southern terrain.

But that's not too much of a problem. Naturally, Southerners on the whole aren't just going to sit around and wait for Hollywood or New York to finance these ideas and then potentially mess them up. Instead, they are exploring and making things happen independently.

Top Pick:
Dirty States of America (2004)
The first documentary to explore the Dirty South culture will likely stand the test of time as one of its best. *Dirty States of America* is an excellent primer that explains various musical styles by region and travels from town to town and city to city to speak with DJs, label owners, producers and artists from all levels of the game. Its fast pace keeps it from being boring or too educational and the original soundtrack (also available on CD) draws on artists from many different areas of the South (highlights come from Killer Mike, David Banner, Bubba Sparxxx, ESG and Lil Flip). The DVD release features uncut interviews with people like Chyna Whyte and Jazze Pha.

Black Spring Break: The Movie (1998)
Written by and starring Daron Fordham ('Southboy'), *Black Spring Break: The Movie* is a hilarious comedy that's kind of a classic among some of my friends, particularly for the bass jam that is its signature, DJ Spanxx's 'Monkey Popping.' The parody of booty clubs and college holidays is not to be missed — but only if you have an appreciation for less-than-professional filmmaking.

Drumline (2002)

Nick Cannon (an actor who is also a budding producer and rapper) stars as a self-taught drummer who joins the drum corps at a fictional Atlanta university (filmed at the real Clark Atlanta University). There's a love story (with actress Zoe Saldana) woven into the plot, but it takes an honest back seat to the numerous drumline scenes that are the backbone of the movie. Rapper Petey Pablo makes a memorable cameo, performing live at the big game. Overall, the film gives non-Southerners a glimpse into the college football and marching band culture that's pure Southern tradition.

Hip-Hop Story 2: Dirty South (2004)

The title of this DVD documentary is somewhat misleading, for it also features a lot of coverage of the Midwest (which, admittedly, isn't totally unrelated). But its most worthwhile bits are the raw concert and club footage of both artist performances and crowds in Miami, Houston and Atlanta. It all expresses more than a narrator could.

I'm Bout It (1997)

Master P's No Limit Records empire truly took off with the release of this straight-to-video movie (now also on DVD), which translated buzz on the streets into a distribution deal with Priority Records and runaway video sales. He would go on to make a few more movies, most notably the comedy *I Got the Hook-Up* (1998), but none with the same cult following. *I'm Bout It* bills itself as a "comedy drama based loosely on [Master P's] life" in the streets of New Orleans. It's also a movie loosely based on any semblance of a script, but is still entertaining – again, with the right attitude in mind. The true scene-stealer in this violent story is Helen Martin (best known for her role as Pearl on the 1980s sitcom *227*), who portrays a blunt-smoking grandma in the best comic relief moment. The *I'm Bout It* soundtrack is also a classic Southern compilation.

Jellybeans (2005)

In production at the time of this writing, this fictional feature from Atlanta-based music producer Dallas Austin (on whose life *Drumline* is loosely based) is about the roller skating rink where he and several of his contemporaries (from TLC to Cee-Lo) used to skate in the 1980s. Famed production trio Organized Noize once had their studio set up there, before they moved into the basement of producer Rico Wade's house and set up the Dungeon Studio. Expect funky flavor and good music from this film.

Lil Jon & The East Side Boyz American Sex Series (2003)

Following in the footsteps of Uncle Luke (who has received sales awards for his *Luke's Peep Show* and *Luke's Freak Fest* DVDs), Lil Jon, Big Sam and Lil Bo take it one step further with a bonafide pornographic DVD that quickly achieved top sales in the urban adult entertainment industry. Certain scenes can be taken straight from almost any typical porn, while others find Lil Jon and the Boyz in the room commenting and directing (but not participating in any actual sex, which keeps their significant others happy). Of course, everything is set to the beats of several of Jon's club hits.

My Life In Idlewild (2005)

Also in production is director Bryan Barber's musical for cable network HBO, a romantic tale based on Andre 3000's *The Love Below* portion of OutKast's multi-platinum *Speakerboxx/The Love Below* double album. Barber's brilliant technicolor videos for the group bode well for their larger budget effort, which is hotly anticipated.

Survival of the Illest (2004)

The plot is a little hard to follow since there's so much blood being shed in this movie, but it's always fun to see rappers in acting situations. Scarface, E-40 and Big Moe appear in this gangster flick set in Houston, which also features several cameos from the Houston hip-hop underground.

Ya Heard Me? (2005)

Named after a common expression in Louisiana, *Ya Heard Me?* (one more in production) is a documentary dedicated to exploring the particular nuances of the music and club culture that has long been going on strong in New Orleans.

RADIO STATIONS

It's difficult to pick a top radio station for a few reasons, including not having the opportunity to fairly sample all that's out there, so I've refrained from doing so. With corporate interests such as Infinity Broadcasting and Clear Channel controlling almost all of the American popular airwaves, there arises a lot of standardization in song playlists that tends to take the personality and local flavor out of a radio station.

Many try to combat their parent company's standardization through a few hours a week of localized programming, so a general rule of thumb is to listen to what a station has to offer on Friday and Saturday nights as well as Sunday mornings. Those are usually the times one might hear local music and content.

College radio stations are also good places to investigate new and emerging sounds. But the programming of specialty shows tends to change semi-frequently, making it not terribly helpful to list specific shows even though certain popular programs tend to last for several years (even beyond the life of a student's career). These stations often transmit on low-power frequencies at the bottom of the spectrum (usually from around 89 to 92 FM), but occasionally are streamed online, enabling them to reach an audience much wider than their small local area. Most cover a spectrum of different kinds of music, but each station listed has at least one hip-hop specialty show.

Alabama

Birmingham:
WBHJ 95.7 FM/95.7 Jamz
http://www.957jamz.com

WBHK 98.7 FM/Kiss
http://www.987kiss.com

Dothan:
WJJN 92.1 FM
http://www.wjjn.greatnow.com/id17.htm

WZND 105.3 FM/105.3 The Beat
http://www.1053thebeat.com

Huntsville:
WHRP 93.3 FM/Power 93.3
http://www.power933.net

WEUP 103.1 FM
http://www.103weup.com

Montgomery:
WZHT 105.7 FM/Hot 105
http://www.myhot105.com

Arkansas

Little Rock:
KABF 88.3 FM
http://www.kabf.org

KIPR 92.3 FM/Power 92.3
http://www.power923.com

KHTE 96.5 FM/Hot 96.5
http://www.hot965.com

Florida

Ft. Myers:
WBTT 105.5 FM/The Beat
http://www.1055thebeat.com

Gainesville:
WTMG 101.3 FM/Magic 101.3
http://www.magic1013.com

Jacksonville:
WHJX 105.7 FM/Hot 105.7
http://www.whjx.biz

Miami:

WVUM 90.5 FM/University of Miami
http://www.wvum.org

WPOW 96.5 FM/Power 96
http://www.power96.com

WEDR 99.1 FM/99Jamz
http://www.wedr.com

WMIB 103.5 FM/The Beat
http://www.thebeatmiami.com

Orlando:

WPRK 91.5 FM/Rollins College
http://www.rollins.edu/wprk

WPYO 95.3 FM/Power 95.3
http://www.power953.com

WJHM 101.9 FM/102 Jamz
http://www.102jamzorlando.com

St. Petersburg:

WILD 98.7 FM/Wild 98.7
http://www.wild987.fm

Tallahassee:

WANM 90.5 FM/Florida A&M
University
http://www.famu.edu/famcast

WBWT 100.7 FM/The Beat
http://www.1007thebeat.com

WWLD 102.3 FM/Blazin' 102.3
http://www.blazin1023.com

Tampa:

WBTP 95.7 FM/95.7 The Beat
http://www.957thebeat.com

Georgia

Atlanta:

WRAS 88.5 FM/Georgia State
University
http://www.wras.org

WREK 91.1 FM/Georgia Tech
http://cyberbuzz.gatech.edu/wrek/

WVEE 103.3 FM/V-103
http://www.v-103.com

WHLE 106.3 FM/Holy Hip-Hop
http://www.live365.com/stations/holy1063
?site=holy1063

WHTA 107.9 FM/Hot 107.9

Augusta:

WFXA 103.1 FM

WPRW 107.7 FM
http://www.power107.net

Macon:

WIBB 97.9 FM
http://www.wibb.com

WFXM 107.1 FM/Foxie 107.1
http://www.foxie107.com

Savannah:
WEAS 93.1 FM/E93
http://www.e93.com

WQBT 94.1 FM
http://www.941thebeat.com

Kentucky

Lexington:
WBTF 107.9 FM/107.9 The Beat
http://www.1079thebeat.com

Louisville:
WGZB 96.5 FM/B-96
http://www.b96jams.com

Louisiana

Baton Rouge:
WEMX 94.1 FM/Max 94.1
http://www.max94one.com

WJNH 107.3 FM/Jam'n 107.3

Grambling:
KGRM 91.5 FM/Grambling University

New Orleans:
WTUL 91.5 FM/Tulane University
http://www.tulane.edu/~wtul/

WQUE 93.3 FM/Q93
http://www.q93.com

KNOU 104.5 FM/Hot 104.5
http://www.hot1045no.com

Shreveport:
KMJJ 99.7 FM
http://www.997kmjj.com

KDKS 102.1 FM

Mississippi

Columbus:
WMSU 92.1 FM/Power 92
http://www.power92fm.net

Jackson:
WJMI 99.7 FM/99 Jams
http://www.wjmi.com

WRJH 97.7 FM/Hot 97.7
http://www.hot977radio.com

North Carolina

Chapel Hill:
WXYC 89.3 FM/University of North
Carolina at Chapel Hill
http://www.wxyc.org

Charlotte:
WPEG 97.9 FM/Power 98
http://www.power98fm.com

Durham:
WXDU 88.7 FM/Duke University
http://www.wxdu.org

WNCU 90.7 FM/North Carolina
Central University
http://www.wncu.org

Fayetteville:
WZFX 99.1 FM/The Fox
http://www.foxy99.com

Greensboro:
WJMH 102.1 FM/102 Jamz
http://www.102jamz.com

Raleigh:
WKNC 88.1 FM/North Carolina State
http://www.wknc.org

Oklahoma

Oklahoma City:
KVSP 1140 AM
http://www.kvsp.com

KKWD 97.9 FM/Wild 97.9
http://www.wild979.com

Tulsa:
KTBT 101.5 FM/101.5 The Beat
http://www.1015thebeat.com

KJMM 105.3 FM/Fresh Jamz 105
http://www.kjmm.com

South Carolina

Charleston:
WWWZ 99.3 FM
http://Z93jamz.com

WWBZ 98.9 FM/Hot 98.9

Clemson:
WSBF 88.1 FM/Clemson University
http://wsbf.clemson.edu

Columbia:
WUSC 80.5 FM/University of South
Carolina at Columbia
http://www.wusc.sc.edu

WHXT 103.9 FM/Hot 103.9
http://www.hot1039fm.com

Tennessee

Chattanooga:
WJTT 94.3 FM/Power 94
http://www.power94.com

Knoxville:
WYIL 98.7 FM/Wild 98.7
http://www.wild987.net

WKHT 104.5 FM/Hot 104.5
http://www.hot1045.net

Memphis:
WHRK 97 FM/K97
http://www.k97fm.com

KXHT 107.1 FM
http://www.hot1071.com

Nashville:
WFSK 88.1 FM/Fisk University
http://www.fisk.edu/wfsk/

WRVU 91.1 FM
http://www.wrvu.org

WUBT 101.1 FM/101 The Beat
http://www.101thebeat.com

WNPL 106.7 FM/Blazin' 106.7

Texas

Amarillo:
KQIZ 93.1 FM
http://www.kqiz.com

Austin:
KVRX 91.7 FM/University of Texas, Austin
http://www.kvrx.org

KDHT 93.3 FM
http://www.hot933.com

Dallas:
KBFB 97.9 FM/97.9 The Beat
http://www.979thebeat.com

KKDA 104.5 FM/K-104
http://www.k104fm.com

Houston:
KTSU 90.9 FM/Texas Southern University
http://www.ktsufm.org

KTRU 91.7 FM/Rice University
http://www.ktru.org

KBXX 97.9 FM/The Box
http://www.kbxx.com

KPTY 104.9 FM/Party 104.9
http://www.party1049.com

Lubbock:
KBTE 104.9 FM
http://www.1049thebeat.com

Tyler:
KBLZ 102.7 FM/The Blaze
http://www.theblaze.cc

GLOSSARY

FEATURING **E-40 Belafonte**

It's stupidly easy to get lost in rhythm and tune out the words of a song, but this music was built on more than just beats. Something as unique as hip-hop deserves an equally innovative lexicon, a semantic scheme that reflects the rule-breaking nature of the culture.

The South is steadily providing hip-hop with semantic and lyrical breakthroughs, not to mention accents and drawls that playfully bend words and cadences in ways that others just can't manage. Words are treated as worthy instruments to assist the voice's tempo, flow and stylistic nuance. This holds true whether it's Pimp C of UGK inventing new words (like *trill*, an extreme form of realness), Scarface boldly hybridizing singing with rapping to formulate his singular delivery, or Big Boi giving the fastest rappers in the game a true run for their money with rapid-fire rhymes on an OutKast tune.

Words are an essential element of hip-hop, not always respected as such. It's amazing to note the range of how rappers treat them. The relationships vary wildly. Some use words like cheap one-night stands that provide the quickest and most basic mode of communication, while others delicately romance words with sweet seduction and tender loving care.

Of course, some people just have more to say. As the most direct descendents of the civil rights movement living in the center of black education in America, Southern rappers on the whole take the power of words seriously.

"I be more hipper than a hippopotamus/Get off in your head like a neurologist ..."
— *E-40, 'SPRINKLE ME'*

"I rap fast but you can quote my rhymes/The greatest game spitter of all time/The most underrated rapper in the game/But everybody want to use my slang ..."
— *E-40, 'WHY THEY DON'T F**K WIT US?'*

He rarely gets proper credit for it, but West Coast rapper and hip-hop mogul E-40 (whose full alias these days is E-40 Belafonte, though many just call him 40,) is one of the most influential linguists of our times. His sayings and words, tilled straight from the soil of Bay Area streets and spiced with his Southern roots, drip with contagion. The urban world has been infected, and the mainstream world now has a slight sneeze and cough.

"The rap game without us is like old folks without bingo," 40 says of the San Francisco Bay Area. "We brought a lot to hip-hop. We're so game *orienfested* out here, we like to use these colorful words. When we pop it, it's really genuine. It's like a hobby for us to do this. And cats, when they get a dose of it, it's like their first hit. They go chasing it; they go chasing that first high. Like their first high, oh man – it stick with 'em for life."

E-40 is one of the great phrase-makers of hip-hop: "Everybody want to use my slang."

Those who follow hip-hop's language closely note that 40 has put out many expressive viruses that others have later developed. 40 doesn't worry so much that people don't necessarily associate all of these sayings with him or his Bay Area colleagues: "I got millions of 'em," he says. People might be able to steal words, but lifting one's imagination is another story altogether. He's preparing his own memoir-tinged dictionary of slang, which will no doubt be a well-studied tome.

Chief among 40's contributions to the language is the *izzle* speech popularized by Snoop Dogg, a form of contracting words in which *fo' shizzle, my nizzle* takes the place of *for sure, my nigga*. In recent years, this became one of mainstream America's favorite things to appropriate from hip-hop and spin out into utterly ridiculous proportions. Snoop himself knew to declare it over once it had made it into a television commercial for the Old Navy clothing company, spilling out of the mouth of Fran Drescher, the comedienne known for her lead role on the 1990s sitcom *The Nanny*.

40 also planted the seeds for a simple phrase that took over hip-hop in the early 1990s: *It's all good*, now associated with the hook on late East Coast rapper Notorious B.I.G.'s debut single 'Juicy.' About the same time he started putting out the saying *poppin' collars*, a snap on the edge of one's shirt to ensure sartorial crispness that 40 devised from watching his grandfather's style of dress. This one took longer to take hold, but rappers, R&B singers, stand-up comics and television personalities have been increasingly poppin' their collars over the last five years.

His expression *you feel me* (to ask for one's understanding) mutated into *you smell me*, which resurfaced as *stank you* and *you're smellcome* by the time Andre 3000 put a spin on it for the OutKast album *Stankonia* in 2000. There are more examples to add to 40's ever growing list; some are hearty little seedlings that will flower in the years to come.

The West Coast holds its firm place in hip-hop history as a trendsetter in slang, but the South is also increasingly recognized as a hotbed of unique words. Unlike so many who have taken their catch phrases from E-40 without attribution, he tries to be as upfront as possible in sharing where he's gotten some of his words. As a pioneer in hip-hop slang, E-40 gives much respect to the South.

"Of course I don't make up all the fuckin' words in the world," he tells *Murder Dog* magazine, "but I make up at least 75 per cent of the shit that I say. The other 25 per cent, I get words from down South, choppin' it up with my folks down South."

40 says the same thing in our interview; in fact, he makes a point to mention the Southern influence and talk about some specific terms.

"Let me definitely let you know that a lot of my words come from the South," he reveals. "Like *acting bad* – 'Man, this boy is acting bad!' – I got that way back in the '90s from my potna [rapper] Mean Green. *Throwed* – 'Man, that boy throwed off in the head.' That's the South all day. *Crunk* needs to be in the dictionary."

Use this glossary to journey from this book out into the general culture of the Dirty South and hip-hop as a whole. For some it's a native tongue established from birth, but for others it will be a glimpse into what can appear to be a coded language. Hopefully, it will help demystify some lyrics or clear up what might have previously seemed an obscure reference. Examine it closely for clues on etymology (the root of a word) and patterns of creation.

Included are words and phrases that have originated in the South as well as those that are rooted in other parts of the country but contribute to the overall hip-hop dialogue. The blend also borrows from car enthusiast lingo, drug terminology, pimp culture and the music industry. Some terms are already out of favor or on the expressway towards becoming outmoded, but exist as time capsules on records you may have yet to discover.

WORD UP!

a & r: Short for "artists and repertoire," a record label executive who finds, signs and develops recording artists.

Alizé: Alizé brand alcohol (cognac and fruit juice blend).

area codes: The telephone area codes to large Southern cities pop up in countless tunes: 404, 770, 678 (Atlanta); 713, 281, 832 (Houston); 305 (Miami); 504 (New Orleans).

ATL: Atlanta.

ATLien: A resident of Atlanta.

A-Town: Atlanta.

A-Town Stomp: Dance created in Atlanta that follows a 1-2-3 rhythm with two small movements or steps and a larger foot stomp on the third beat. Listen to: TLC's 'Come Get 'Some,' Usher's 'Yeah.'

baller: Originally created to describe the wealth of professional athletes, now refers to someone with money and clout.

bama: Derogatory term meaning backward or from the country (and, according to the *Hip-Hoptionary* by Alonzo Westbrook, a shortening of Alabama).

bird: Cocaine.

Bankhead bounce: A dance created in the Bankhead area of Atlanta where the shoulders move sharply up and down while the arms and body pivot slightly. Listen to: Diamond & D-Roc's 'Bankhead Bounce.'

The Bay: San Francisco Bay Area.

BET: Black Entertainment Television.

Belvedere: Brand of vodka.

Big Easy: New Orleans, Louisiana.

Bishop/Bishop Magic Don Juan: Famed Chicago pimp turned 'spiritual advisor' to rappers, frequently appearing on stage, videos and records. Listen to: 'Area Codes,' by Ludacris featuring Nate Dogg's, Twista featuring 8Ball, and 'Pimp On' by Bishop Don Magic Juan and Too $hort'.

bitch-ass nigga: Extreme insult to one's manhood.

bling/bling bling: Created to describe the gleam of diamond, platinum and gold, it has been extended to refer to any part of a luxury lifestyle. Listen to: BG's 'Bling Bling.'

blow: Nickname for cocaine.

blow up: To become big or popular.

blunt: Marijuana cigar constructed out of tobacco leaves. Named after the Phillies Blunts brand of cigar.

boo: Term of endearment.

booty: 1. A butt. 2. Term to describe the sexually explicit bass music popularized by 2 Live Crew.

bounce: 1. Literally, to bounce up and down (as on the dancefloor) 2. A style of music originated in New Orleans, blending bass and hip-hop elements with regional rhythms like zydeco.

bout it/I'm bout it: To represent; literally "to be about it." Listen to: Master P's 'I'm Bout It.'

Bruce Bruce: Popular African-American comedian from Atlanta who has hosted various programs on BET and been immortalized in several songs. Listen to: Too $hort featuring Lil Jon''s 'Shake That Monkey,' Silk The Shocker''s 'We Like Dem Girls,' and Ying Yang Twins' 'Salt Shaker.'

cake: Money.

cee-lo/c-lo: 1. Dice game. 2. Recording artist Cee-Lo.

chickenheads: Girls who appear to have little going for themselves and want a man for his money and status. Sometimes referred to as *pigeons*, or *scrubs* (for men). Listen to: Project Pat's 'Chickenheads.'

choosin': Originally meaning prostitutes selecting their pimps, it now has been incorporated into a more general form of date speak. Listen to Too $hort featuring Jazze Pha's 'Choosin'.'

Chopper City: New Orleans, Louisiana.

chronic: Strong marijuana.

click/clique: One's crew of friends and associates.

College Park: Neighborhood in Southwest Atlanta often name-checked by Ludacris.

coochie: Pussy.

coochie poppin'/pop that coochie: Crowd-pleasing technique favored by strippers in which they make their private parts pulsate. See also: monkey popping, P-poppin', pussy pop, pussy popping. Listen to: 2 Live Crew's 'Pop That Coochie,' DJ Spanxx's 'Monkey Popping,' and Ludacris' 'P-Poppin'.'

Cris/Crissy: Louis Roederer Cristal champagne, one of hip-hop's most coveted luxury brands.

crunk/get crunk: 1. To have or create energy. 2. Youth culture and musical movement popularized by Lil Jon & the East Side Boyz and Ying Yang Twins in Atlanta.

crunk juice: Grey Goose brand vodka and Lil Jon's CRUNK!!! brand energy drink.

cut/cutting: Fuck/fucking.

dime: 1. A hot girl (also *dimepiece*). 2. A *dimebag* of marijuana, an increasingly antiquated unit that once cost $10.

Dirty South/dirty dirty: The South.

don't get it twisted: Make no mistake.

drank: Nickname for *syrup*.

dro: Nickaname for *hydro*.

drop-top: A convertible.

ducats: Money.

Dutch Masters: Brand of cigar used to make blunts.

eightball/8ball: 1. 3.5 grams of cocaine 2. Rapper 8Ball

faded: 1. Intoxicated. 2. Tired.

fa'sho: For sure.

floss/flossing: To show off.

40: 1. A malt liquor beverage containing 40 ounces of liquor. 2. Rapper E-40.

Freaknik: Now defunct annual spring break party in Atlanta meant for students attending schools in the AUC (Atlanta University Center) to celebrate that attracted national visitors and, to put it mildly, risqué behavior.

fronts: Gold or platinum tooth coverings.

game/the game: Originally coined to describe the 'industry' of pimping, it has been appropriated in hip-hop to describe the music industry.

ganja: Marijuana.

gentleman's club: Adult nightclub.

Georgia dome: 1. Atlanta's Georgia Dome sports arena 2. Oral sex. Listen to: Ying Yang Twins' 'GA Dome.'

gold album: Certification awarded to albums that sell in excess of 500,000 copies in America.

grippin' grain: Fancy wood-grain steering wheels on cars.

gully/gutter: From the streets.

H-Town: Houston, Texas.

Hanh!: An exclamation made famous by D-Roc of the Ying Yang Twins that he uses to punctuate sentences. Listen to: Ying Yang Twins' 'Hanh.'

head buster/bussa: Someone ready to fight; literally, to "bust a head open." Listen to: Soulja Slim's 'Head Buster,' Lil Scrappy's 'Head Bussa.'

Hen: Hennessy brand cognac.

Hip/Hipnotiq: Hipnotiq brand alcohol (cognac blended with fruit juice).

ho: Whore, loose woman.

Hoody-hoo!: An exclamation shouted out to call in backup assistance in fighting situations, made briefly famous by Master P and protégé TRU. Listen to: TRU's 'Hoody-Hoo.'

hook: The memorable part of a song's chorus.

hydro: Marijuana grown hydroponically (without soil in nutrient-enriched water).

ice: Diamonds. Also *iced out*, to describe something studded with diamonds.

ice cream: Crack cocaine. Listen to: Master P's 'Ice Cream Man.'

I'mma: Contraction of "I'm going to."

jimmy: Penis.

jimmy hat: Condom.

joint: Marijuana cigarette.

jump out: Police in unmarked cars.

keys (ki's): A kilogram of cocaine.

knuck: 1. Knuckles. 2. To fight.

l: Blunt.

'Lac: Cadillac.

lean: Nickname for *syrup.*

Liberty City: One of the most economically

disadvantaged neighborhoods of Miami, Florida, which also produced music stars Luther Campbell, Trick Daddy, Trina and Jacki-O.

lock-down: Jail.

Magic City: Miami.

Magnolia: Magnolia Housing Projects in New Orleans, Louisiana.

MARTA: Metropolitan Atlanta Rapid Transit Authority, Atlanta's public transportation company.

Mary Jane: Marijuana.

MIA: Miami.

mixtape: CD or tape containing songs normally by a variety of artists used in hip-hop to promote new and uncensored music.

Mo: Moët champagne.

Mom and Pop: An independently owned store.

Most High: God.

nann: No/none. Listen to Trick Daddy's 'Nann Nigga.'

n'em: Contraction of 'and them.'

nine/9: 9 millimeter pistol.

N.O.: New Orleans.

Orange Mound: Neighborhood of Memphis, Tennessee where 8Ball & MJG grew up.

P-Funk: Music style created by George Clinton (a union of his groups Parliament-Funkadelic).

p-poppin'/pussy pop/pussy popping: See *coochie poppin'*.

paper: Money.

peace up, A-Town down: Phrase describing two hand gestures. Holding the index and middle finger up in a V means *peace*, and flipping them down forms an A for *Atlanta*.

pimp: A 'manager' of prostitutes.

pimp cup: A drinking goblet favored by pimps, popularized by Lil Jon with his silver, jewel-encrusted cups.

platinum album: Certification awarded to albums that sell in excess of 1,000,000 copies in America.

po-po: Police.

popped: 1. Killed. 2. Picked up by police.

potna: Partner.

QP: A quarter-pound of marijuana.

RIAA: Recording Industry Association of America.

rims: Car tire rims.

runner: 1. Loose woman, slut. 2. Someone who transports drugs.

screw/screwed/screwed and chopped: Pioneered by the late DJ Screw in Houston, Texas, *screw* originated as a technique of manipulating records by adjusting the pitch control and scratching in beats, words and sounds that sound chopped up. Now, some artists release special *screwed and chopped* versions of their albums in which each song is remixed in this method.

scrubs: Male *chickenheads*.

shawty/shorty: 1. Term of affection for a girl. 2. Little kid.

shoes: Car tires and rims.

'Sip: Mississippi.

16 bars: Unit of musical measurement that rappers typically receive to perform on a guest spot on someone else's song. One bar equals four beats of music.

Sizzurp: 1. Nickname for *syrup*. 2. Brand name for a purple punch liqueur developed by New York rap crew The Diplomats.

skeet: Lil Jon has been polite about this term, saying on the Kings of Crunk DVD that it means "to expel fluid." Let's keep it real and tell you that it means to ejaculate. Listen to: Lil Jon & the East Side Boyz featuring Ying Yang Twins' 'Get Low.'

spit: To rap.

stunna: Someone who stands out and shows off. Listen to: Baby's '#1 Stunna.'

SWAT: Acronym for Southwest Atlanta.

Swisher Sweets: Brand of cigar often used to make a blunt. Forms basis of *swisha*, as in Texas record label Swisha House.

syrup: An intoxicant popularized in Texas whose effects serve to slow the user's world down. Recipes vary as to one's access to ingredients, but the standard concoction mixes codeine cough syrup (which is supposed to be available only by doctor's prescription) with a soda like Sprite on ice and maybe a Jolly Rancher hard fruit candy thrown in for extra sweetness. See also: *Drank, lean, sizzurp*. Listen to: Three 6 Mafia's 'Sippin' On Syrup,' Big Moe's 'Purple Stuff.'

2-way: Short for "2-way pager," a wireless electronic device that allows for the exchange of text messages.

teenage rims: An insult signifying a lack of wealth, referring to car tire rims that measure 16 or 18 inches.

Third Coast: A term for the South in hip-hop dialogue, some find it to be a back-handed term (as they might dislike *Dirty South* for its unclean connotation).

throwin' bows: To move one's elbows around wildly, almost in a form of air-punch. The expression came out out of Atlanta clubs as part of the crunk movement.

throwed: Messed up or intoxicated.

trap: Area where drugs are sold. Listen to: T.I.'s 'Trap Muzik.'

trill: Triple real, or truly real.

20s/22s/24s: Refers to the size of car tire rims as measured in inches — if someone is "rollin' on 22s," they have 22-inch rims on their tires. Also a handy way to date a song, for 22s and 24s have only come into play in the last few years.

twerk/twurk: To dance and move suggestively, as strippers do. Listen to: Ying Yang Twins' 'Whistle (While You Twurk).'

vogues: Car tire rims.

whoadie: New Orleans expression referring to a familiar man or woman.

yac/yak/'gnac: Cognac.

Ya heard me?: Do you understand?

Yay Area: San Francisco Bay Area.

yeek: An old-school dance style popular in the early days of Atlanta hip-hop.

youngblood: A young person.

young buck: 1. A young person. 2. Recording artist Young Buck.

188

BIBLIOGRAPHY

Alexander, Phalon (Jazze Pha). Original interview with author, October 2004.

Benton, Stanley (Stat Quo). Original interview with author, July 2004.

Bogdanov, Vladimir; Woodstra, Chris; Erlewine, Stephen Thomas; Bush, John (editors). *All Music Guide to Hip-Hop* (Backbeat Books, 2003).

Bray, Daika. 'Chingo Bling,' online interview with *Murder Dog* (www.murderdog.com).

Bridges, Chris (Ludacris). Original interview with author, April 2003.

Brown, David (Young Buck). Original interview with author, August 2004.

Callaway, Thomas (Cee-Lo). Original interviews with author, December 2003 and July 2004.

Campbell, Luther. Original interview with author, July 2004.

Creekmur, Chuck. 'The Empire Strikes Back,' *Vibe*, December 2004.

Crump, Lavell (David Banner). Original interview with author, October 2004.

Flex (director). *Lyricist Lounge: Dirty States of America* (Image Entertainment, 2004).

Foxx, Felisha. 'Jam Pony Express,' *Ozone*, July 2004.

Goodwin, Marlon Jermaine (MJG). Original interview with author, September 2004.

Hardnett, Wayne (Bone Crusher). Original interview with author, August 2004.

Jackson, Eric Ron (Kaine, Ying Yang Twins). Original interview with author, September 2004.

Kohn, Angela (Jacki-O). Original interview with author, July 2004.

Ladd, Donna. 'Tough Questions for David Banner,' *Jackson Free Press*, May 15, 2003.

Martin, Stephanie (Chyna Whyte). Original interview with author, June 2004.

Mumbi Moody, Nekesa. 'BET Provides More "Exposure" for Videos,' *Associated Press*, April 7, 2004.

Neal, Wendell (Lil Bo, East Side Boyz). Original interview with author, September 2004.

Norris, Sam (Big Sam, East Side Boyz). Original interview with author, September 2004.

Oh, Minya. 'Bling Bling Added to Oxford English Dictionary,' MTV Online (www.mtv.com), April 30, 2003.

Palmer, Robert. *Rock & Roll: An Unruly History* (Harmony Books, 1995).

Penrice, Ronda Racha. 'Pole Vaulting to Success,' *Creative Loafing*, July 22-28, 2004.

Reeves, Mosi. 'Anatomy of a Hit,' *Miami New Times*, January 1, 2004.

Sandimanie, Bobby (I-20). Original interview with author, August 2004

Sarig, Roni. 'Dungeon Family Tree,' *Creative Loafing*, September 18, 2003.

Sarig, Roni. 'Cash Flow,' *Scratch*, Winter 2005.

Smith, Jonathan (Lil Jon). Original interview with author, May 2004.

Smith, Premro (8Ball). Original interview with author, September 2004.

Shaw, Todd (Too $hort). Original interview with author, August 2004.

Stevens, Earl (E-40). Original interview with author, October 2004.

Thompson, Dave. *Third Ear: Funk* (Backbeat Books, 2001).

Toop, David. *Rap Attack* (Pluto Press, 1984).

Vincent, Rickey. *Funk: The Music, The People, and The Rhythm of the One* (St. Martin's Griffin, 1996).

Westbrook, Alonzo T. *Hip-Hoptionary* (Broadway Books, 2002).

INDEX OF ARTISTS

ACKNOWLEDGEMENTS

I'm very grateful to Denise Sullivan, Tom Maffei, Aunt Kizzy and the memorable brunch in Inglewood that led to this book!

Thank you Arlene and (Lil) Ron Palmer for believing in this project and me. Thanks to Missy Buchanan for the research assistance, for dealing with a roommate with a first book and a crazy deadline and for being my surrogate Southerner way out West.

Terry Black: Thanks for the miles!!

Thank you 8Ball and MJG, Bone Crusher, Luther Campbell, Cee-Lo, I-20, Jacki-O, Lil Jon & the East Side Boyz, Ludacris, Jazze Pha, Stat Quo, Chyna Whyte, Ying Yang Twins and Young Buck for your insightful interviews and faith. Extra respect to Too $hort and E-40 for that down home Yay Area love.

Bless you, David Banner, for sharing your time and a great Foreword. Thanks to Julia Beverly for making it happen at the 11th hour as well as having a camera pretty much everywhere someone could want.

To the behind-the-scenes folks who help make these artists shine, I appreciate your time and help on this book:

Richie Abbott, Nicole Balin, Betsy Bolte, David Bosch, Sasha Brookner, Jeff Chennault, Jeff Ciminera, Derrick Crooms, Dennis Dennehy, Tony Edwards, José Fendrick (aka ZEEK), Laura Giles, Damika Jordan, Siri Khalsa, Roberta Magrini, Giovanna Melchiorre, Ticeman Merriweather, Greg Miller, KC Morton, Embry Rucker, Tresa Sanders, Barry Underhill, Joe Wiggins.

Cheers to the Backbeat Books crew in London, Cheltenham and Bristol for taking this adventure with me and not complaining too loudly about how long it took. From the American South to South of the Thames, this is truly an international story and I'm glad to have found fellow music lovers with whom to tell it.

These fine folks provided direct assistance and tips for the book, or offered particularly helpful life support along the way:

Andy Shih, A.V. Williams, Cherie Miller, Craig Roseberry, Diana Baron, Ethan Jenkins, Greg Jacobs, Griffy2K (and Temptation from College Park), Flogging Mousie, Gunnar Hissam, Jenn Leibhart, Kevin Dowell, Kieran Wyatt, Kurt B. Reighley, Lee Howard, Lily Moayeri, Liz Morentin, Lynn Hasty, Maggie Stein (thanks for the crunktro), Michael Paoletta, Mosi Reeves, Nat Illumine, Nick Doherty, Nicole Powers, Paul D. Miller, Raymond Leon Roker, Scott Sterling, Sean Bidder, Simon Rust Lamb, DJ Smallz, Stacy Osbaum, Tamara Warren, Tim Barr, Trent Buckroyd, Trevor Seamon, Wron G.

PICTURE CREDITS

2-3 Courtesy of KOCH; 6 Julia Beverly; 21 Courtesy of Bad Boy Records; 24 Embry Rucker; 28, 32, 36, 38, 43, 48 Julia Beverly; 53 Tamara Palmer; 57 Julia Beverly; 63 Courtesy of BMG; 68 Julia Beverly; 73 Jonathan Mannion/Courtesy of Capitol Records; 77 Julia Beverly; 83 Desmond/Courtesy of Grown Man Music; 88 Tamara Palmer; 91 Joe Wiggins; 100 Desmond/Courtesy of Grown Man Music; 105 Julia Beverly; 112 Courtesy of Big Chile Enterprises; 114, 117, 120, 139, 144 Julia Beverly; 150 Courtesy of KOCH; 154 Julia Beverly; 157 Courtesy of KOCH; 158 Barry Underhill; 163 Courtesy of KOCH; 182 Courtesy of Jive Records.